Supporting Gifted and Talented Pupils in the Secondary School

Moira Thomson has been Principal Teacher Support for Learning at Broughton High School Edinburgh for more than 30 years.

At the same time, she has been a Development Officer with the City of Edinburgh Department of Children and Families since 1999. She has been involved in the development of the City's Guidelines for Gifted and Talented Pupils; in advising schools and colleagues about gifted education; and in the delivery of Continuing Professional Development on Gifted Education to colleagues. In 2002, whilst exploring strategies to combat underachievement in gifted pupils, she became the founding Coordinator of Edinburgh's Gifted and Talented summer programme.

She was appointed an Associate Tutor with the Scottish Network for Able Pupils in 1999 after completing the Glasgow University Master's Module in Educating More Able Pupils. This role has involved sharing good practice nationally; devising programmes and developing materials for gifted education; and advising schools locally about initiatives and developments for educating gifted pupils on a wider scale.

Well known in Scotland for contributions to the support of dyslexic pupils at the secondary school, and membership of the Scottish Parliament's cross party working group on dyslexia, she is in demand as a speaker at events around the country and abroad.

Supporting Gifted and Talented Pupils in the Secondary School

Moira Thomson

P·C·P

Paul Chapman
Publishing

To all the gifted young people with whom I have had the
privilege of working

First published 2006

Paul Chapman Publishing
A SAGE Publications Company
1 Oliver's Yard
55 City Road
London EC1Y 1SP

SAGE Publications Inc
2455 Teller Road
Thousand Oaks, California 91320

SAGE Publications India Pvt Ltd
B-42, Panchsheel Enclave
Post Box 4109
New Delhi 110 017

Library of Congress Control Number: 2006901648
A catalogue record for this book is available from the British Library

ISBN-10 1-4129-1967-3   ISBN-13 978-1-4129-1967-8
ISBN-10 1-4129-1968-1   ISBN-13 978-1-4129-1968-5 (pbk)

Typeset by C&M Digitals (P) Ltd., Chennai, India
Printed on paper from sustainable resources
Printed and bound in Great Britain by Cromwell Press Ltd, Trowbridge, Wiltshire

Contents

Acknowledgements

I would like to thank:

Professeur Françoys Gagné, for permission to include his developmental model of giftedness and talent (DMGT) 2003 (pp. 4–5) and for the use of his notes.

Tudor Morris, Director of Music at the City of Edinburgh Music School for his notes about the Music School (pp. 106–08).

Lesley Riddell, Education Manager, The Lighthouse, Glasgow for her article and for permission to include the 'Fantasy Design Workshop: Design a Portable Kitchen' (pp. 86–8).

Belle Wallace for permission to include the TASC Wheel (p. 51), and for her support and encouragement in this project.

Also Kate Russell, Mary Farrell and Pearl McKay and their pupils for their contributions.

I would also like to thank the following for patiently answering my questions, providing information and advice:

Keith Falconer, Senior Executive, Creative Futures Team, Scottish Enterprise Glasgow.

Lindsey Fraser, Director, the Pushkin Prizes.

Professor Miraca U.M. Gross, Director, Gifted Education Research, Resource and Information Centre (GERRIC), the University of New South Wales.

Gerry Toner, Programme Director, SCHOLAR Programme, Heriot-Watt University.

Rae Galbraith, Scottish Network for Able Pupils at Glasgow University.

And to:

Lesley Johnston, Maureen Brice, Chris Smith and Margaret Sutherland for their encouragement, advice and support.

Becky Leach for adding her personal comments to the 'Pushkin Prizes' case study.

Jude Bowen for making this book a reality.

Part I

Identification and Provision

Chapter 1

Defining Giftedness

This chapter looks at:

- Definitions of giftedness
- Françoys Gagné's differentiated model of giftedness and talent
- The role of the teacher
- A school-based definition

The term 'gifted' is frequently used to describe abilities demonstrated in sport or in the creative arts – 'a gifted athlete', 'a gifted actor' and so on. These references often apply to a specific ability, and may imply that this ability has appeared without systematic learning or teaching, and that those possessing such 'gifts' have somehow been endowed with their particular ability in a way that is beyond the control or scope of education, despite clear indications that the 'gifted' individuals have usually spent years honing their skills.

A number of terms are commonly used by teachers to describe 'gifted' pupils: bright, talented, high flier, exceptionally able, brilliant (George, 1995, 1997; Wallace, 2000). Teachers use these terms interchangeably to refer to pupils who have demonstrated particular abilities and for whom different educational provision is needed.

One definition is that *gifted* pupils have the potential to demonstrate superior performance in a number of areas, and *talented* refers to those who do this in a single area (George, 2000). Eyre's (1997) multi-dimensional view of giftedness is a more complex one and she considers that 'gifted and talented' describes not only those with high academic abilities, but should also include those with musical, sporting or artistic ability.

Most definitions of giftedness in secondary school pupils refer to their abilities and achievements in particular areas, fitting the popular theory of multiple intelligences (Gardner, 1993) indicating different kinds of 'giftedness'.

The English definition of 'gifted' learners as those who have abilities in one or more academic subjects and 'talented' learners as those displaying abilities in sport, music, design or creative arts is not universally accepted by researchers and educators, even across the United Kingdom. In Scotland, teachers often use 'more able' when referring to their highest achieving pupils (McMichael, 1998), while the Welsh Assembly used 'more able and talented' in their 2003 *Guidance for Local Education Authorities*.

In New Zealand giftedness is defined in terms of learning characteristics indicating the possession of special abilities that give pupils the potential to achieve outstanding performance (Riley et al., 2004). No specific definition of giftedness is given, but, as in many other 'national' guidance publications, schools are expected to develop their own definitions based on the published principles.

Most teachers would agree that gifted pupils are those who require greater breadth and depth of learning activities and extended opportunities across the curriculum in order to develop their abilities. The learning needs required by some pupils to develop their abilities is fully illustrated by Gagné's (1985, 2003a) differentiated model of giftedness and talent (DMGT) (see Figure 1.1). In this, Gagné proposes that giftedness is the potential or aptitude within an individual, and that this can be developed into talent (developed abilities or high performance) by environmental and other factors.

This model explores what an individual needs to do in order to transform an aptitude into a developed skill. Gagné clearly defines giftedness as 'natural' abilities that may be made apparent through the ease and rate at which individuals acquire new skills – learning appears to be easier and faster in individuals whose natural abilities are high, but these aptitudes must pass through a developmental process before they can be demonstrated as 'talents' (systematically developed skills). Talent development requires systematic learning and practising, and the more intensive these activities are, the greater the demonstrated skills will be. In the DMGT, while one cannot be talented without first being gifted, it is possible for natural abilities not to be translated into talents, so that academic underachievement of some intellectually gifted pupils may be linked to a failure to engage fully in the developmental process.

ROLE OF THE TEACHER

What makes Gagné's model particularly meaningful to teachers is the place given to the developmental process of learning, training and practice combined with environmental and intrapersonal catalysts which transform natural aptitudes into skills that can be publicly demonstrated. In sport, for example, coaches assess those athletes most likely to attain high levels of performance using not only natural abilities but also catalysts like intrinsic motivation, competitiveness, persistence and personality, while sports organisations provide the best environmental conditions to foster athletes' development. Even chance plays a role! No matter how much natural ability a young athlete may have, and no matter how well trained and motivated (even with the very best of coaching and equipment), if the international selector does not see him perform, he may never attain at the highest levels. However, the teacher/trainer/coach will always try to ensure that protégées are given every opportunity to shine – and most of them will go to great lengths to eliminate chance as a factor that might prevent this.

In the DMGT, teachers are able to see a clear role for themselves in the transformation of natural aptitudes into developed skills. Learning implies a role for the teacher in devising programmes for pupils to follow in order to

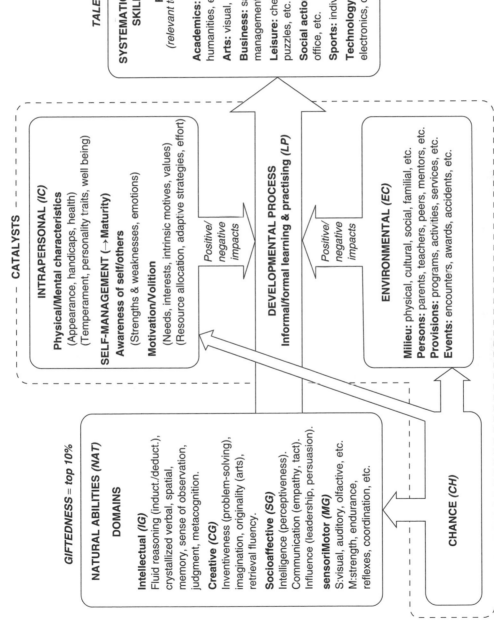

Figure 1.1   Gagne's Differentiated Model of Giftedness and Talent (DGMT, US, 2003)

develop and improve their skills, while practice is undertaken by pupils themselves and linked to motivation and environmental circumstances, though supported by teachers through the provision of resources. Teachers can provide a motivating classroom environment by creating conditions that sustain, guide and enhance a pupil's inherent motivation to learn; they can stimulate pupils' interests and create a climate that promotes achievement by helping pupils accept and value their gifts; and they can provide resources that do not place limits on individual pupils' attainments.

SCHOOL-BASED DEFINITION

Gifted educational provision in school may be a systematic form of intervention designed to foster the process of talent development in pupils. Such intervention does not depend on teachers' adherence to any particular definition of giftedness, but is built on the awareness that some pupils are gifted and that the teacher's role is to support their development.

Schools need to develop a definition of giftedness that:

- allows the recognition of both performance and potential;
- recognises that pupils may be gifted in one or more areas;
- reflects a 'multiple intelligences' approach that includes a range of special abilities;
- acknowledges that gifted and talented pupils demonstrate exceptionality in relation to their age-peers of similar backgrounds;
- provides for differentiated educational opportunities for gifted and talented pupils, including social and emotional support.

No matter what definition of 'gifted' is accepted, teachers need to see their own role in working with gifted pupils, and this may sometimes be obscured by the multiplicity of definitions.

The search for an absolute definition of giftedness to apply to pupils in the secondary school may be rooted in the fact that many gifted pupils have abilities that are not evident within the context of the school curriculum, so teachers are not in a position to create opportunities and offer experiences that promote a developmental process to enable these pupils to develop their skills. Some pupils allow the teacher only glimpses of their potential or ability, suggesting that appropriate educational provision for all in an inclusive setting might be necessary to encourage the most able to reveal themselves (Wallace, 2000).

📖 FURTHER READING

Colangelo, N. and Davis, G.A. (eds) (2003), *Handbook of Gifted Education*, 3rd edn. Boston, MD: Allyn and Bacon

Gross, M.U.M., MacLeod, B. and Pretorius, M. (2001) *Gifted Students in Secondary Schools Differentiating the Curriculum*, 2nd edn. Sydney, Australia: Gerric

Renzulli, J.S. (1999) What is this thing called giftedness, and how do we develop it? A twenty-five year perspective', *Journal for the Education of the Gifted*, 23 (1): 3–54

Sternberg, R.J. and Davidson, J. (eds) (1986) *Conceptions of Giftedness*. New York: Cambridge University Press

Chapter 2

Identification of Giftedness

This chapter looks at:

- Identification procedures
  - through provision
  - teacher nomination
  - profiling
  - standardised tests
  - checklists
  - rating scales
- References for checklists and standardised tests
- Sources of identification checklists
- Example of a checklist

Some people consider that identification of individual children as gifted is elitist, yet these children are elite in the same way as anyone who becomes an Olympic medallist, a solo performer or a leader.

Generally, gifted pupils are thought to share common elements (Gross et al., 2001) such as the potential for unusually high performance and a capacity to think clearly, analytically and evaluatively. Identification of giftedness should be a flexible, continuous process that combines the assessment of '*precocious achievement or behaviour*' with the creation of conditions that will '*allow giftedness to develop and reveal itself*' (Eyre 2002a). In order to ensure that gifted pupils are given every opportunity for this to happen, and to prevent disadvantage on the basis of cultural, socio-economic background or disability, identification processes should be able to be carried out within an inclusive educational setting.

The responsibility for identifying gifted pupils lies with the school, specifically with individual teachers. Many teachers are fully aware that actual performance is not always an indicator of giftedness, so schools should establish a range of procedures for identifying gifted pupils that include methods designed to discover potential or ability not revealed by current performance. A range of approaches should be used to assess the ability or potential of pupils at the secondary school. Eyre (1997) lists information from the primary schools, tests and classroom observation; Freeman (1998) highlights teacher nomination, parent and peer recommendation and intelligence; while George (2000) includes tests of achievement and creativity along with checklists and rating scales.

IDENTIFICATION THROUGH PROVISION

Schools should have procedures in place for revealing pupil ability (Eyre, 2002a) and foster the emergence of individual pupils' gifts and talents, including classroom environments that encourage creative, divergent and higher-level thinking with an open-ended approach to learning (Renzulli, 1999).

There may be difficulty in identifying gifted pupils with hidden potential; Freeman (2000) discusses a 'sports approach' that allows pupils to excel within the context of what is available to them – they could choose for themselves whether to participate and at what level. The benefits of using this approach to identify pupils' abilities are:

- it is process-based and continuous;
- it uses multiple criteria;
- it could be validated for every course of action and provision;
- pupils' abilities could be presented as a profile with the next learning stages identified;
- attitudes, possibly affected by influences such as culture and gender, could be taken into account in the profile.

TEACHER NOMINATION

There is a general perception among teachers that gifted pupils are those who do things earlier, faster or better compared to their age peers. There may be considerable discrepancy between a teacher's subjective judgement and the results of objective tests (Freeman, 1998) and research indicates that, while teachers consistently identify gifted pupils, they tend to pick the same type of pupil, choosing those who conform to their expectations, often identifying pupils according to their way of working rather than cognitive ability, thereby sometimes underestimating the actual ability level of those identified while missing others completely. At the secondary school, where ability is often considered to be subject specific, teachers tend to be more accurate in their identification of pupils who are gifted in particular areas of the curriculum.

Pupils who do things differently from others are not always considered gifted by their teachers, as they are often not 'model' pupils and may present considerable challenges within the classroom. George (2000) distinguishes between 'bright' and 'gifted' children: the bright child responds in a way that conforms to the teacher's expectations, while the gifted child might ask awkward questions, sometimes challenge the teacher, perhaps draw inferences and reach conclusions without going through the various stages laid down in the lesson plan. It is not possible to determine how a teacher's mental image of a 'gifted pupil' influences identification (Freeman, 1998), so subjective decisions will always be open to question. The apparent preference of teachers for bright, easy-to-teach pupils, who may fit some predetermined stereotype, is one reason why parents, pupils – and teachers themselves – often require additional information or evidence to support any identification of individuals as gifted.

PROFILING

Primary school teachers have to summarise when passing on information to the secondary school, so important indications of specific ability may be missed, and some secondary subject teachers may not give appropriate weight to primary teachers' comments, assuming that since there has been little specialist teaching in their subject those pupils will have little acquired skill. It is important for secondary teachers to recognise that the attainment levels of pupils passed on by primary colleagues will reflect only the level at which they were assessed, and that this may not be the same as the level at which they are capable of performing, so additional information should be sought at the transition stage.

The primary school might produce a profile of each gifted pupil and make this available to the secondary school before transfer. This profile might include:

- standardised test results (including IQ tests);
- examples of work and targets achieved;
- anecdotal evidence relating to performance;
- information about the pupil's preferred learning style;
- checklists of behaviours;
- self-assessments and personal inventories of interests;
- details of successful teaching/learning strategies;
- observations of the pupil in different learning environments;
- details of non-curricular achievements;
- psychological reports.

Any profile should be shared with parents so that they may contribute information about out-of-school activities and achievements. It must be recognised that a fully developed profile containing all of the information listed above is unlikely to exist unless the pupil has already been identified as exceptional. Since it is generally accepted that high abilities may be identified in pupils at any stage, profiling procedures should be available for use with pupils throughout secondary education.

STANDARDISED TESTS

Teacher reports, parents' anecdotes and checklists may contribute significantly to the identification of gifted pupils, and could be used to decide whether there should be further investigation of ability and attainment. Standardised tests are objective screening measures and, when used in conjunction with subjective measures, may provide a comprehensive assessment to support identification of giftedness. This combination has the added advantage of enabling teachers to identify gifted pupils who may be underachieving. Many schools use standardised achievement tests, measuring attainment in literacy or mathematics and other subjects in the secondary curriculum. However, some standardised tests have a ceiling, so pupils whose scores lie in the top 10 per cent for their age group should be retested using tests for older groups in order to gain a clearer indication of actual attainment.

Tests of intellectual or cognitive ability might also be used, but schools should consider using these tests only when the pupil's level of ability is in doubt or when underachievement is a concern, to avoid boredom and deteriorating results. Tests designed to measure specific abilities and/or creativity may be an appropriate form of identification/assessment where there is a history of difficulties that may have masked ability over a period of time.

Standardised test scores should not be the only evidence used to identify giftedness, which is more than just intellectual precocity (Gross, 2004), so a range of different types of evidence should be used. *Details of some tests of cognitive or specific abilities are listed at the end of this chapter.*

CHECKLISTS

Teachers' observation of their pupils in a variety of contexts has contributed to the development of the use of checklists or inventories of specific characteristics and/or behaviours. These checklists are commonly used to collect evidence of pupils' giftedness, supplemented by a plethora of assessment instruments, inventories of interests, and questionnaires.

Most checklists offer a list of characteristics or behaviours that a gifted pupil would demonstrate, though a pupil need not be rated as outstanding in all of these, but there would probably be indications of:

- rapid learning;
- excellent memory;
- outstanding problem-solving and reasoning ability;
- persistent intellectual curiosity;
- ability to see subtle relationships;
- a wide range of interests;
- mature and unusual vocabulary;
- ability to sustain concentration;
- responsibility and independence in class work;
- initiative and originality;

- flexible thinking;

- ability to consider problems from different aspects;

- observant nature and responsiveness to new ideas;

- ability to communicate with adults in a mature way;

- enjoyment of intellectual challenges;

- subtle, sometimes quirky sense of humour.

This is not a definitive list of the characteristics that describe gifted pupils, and teachers should consult a range of lists available (see 'Sources of identification checklists' later in this chapter) and then follow the advice of George (1995) who proposes that they construct and validate their own checklists. It is important to remember that not all gifted pupils will demonstrate all the items on a checklist, and there may be some characteristics of giftedness which are not obvious in school because the provision available does not allow them to emerge.

RATING SCALES

A rating scale might be used when teachers need to place a pupil on a continuum and discriminate between levels of giftedness of pupils in subject areas. Since gifted pupils cannot be regarded as one homogeneous group, within any group identified there could still be a wide range of ability (Gross, 2004). Teachers may need ways of discriminating between these pupils otherwise profoundly and exceptionally gifted pupils may be at risk of not being identified. Rating scales, like checklists, should be complied in schools in order to make specific discriminations between pupils in order to ensure that provision is being made in the most appropriate way for individual pupils. Categories of gifted pupils that might be considered when using rating scales include high achievers who:

- identify themselves by the quantity and quality of their responses or activities;

- demonstrate outstanding ability or talent in one or more areas;

- outstrip their peers but may fall behind due to decreased motivation, a change of teacher or learning environment;

- demonstrate strengths (as opposed to giftedness) in all academic areas.

Those less likely to be identified:

- sit quietly, get on with their work and complete set tasks;

- appear shy and reticent – even isolated;

- seldom ask questions because they understand concepts and tasks immediately;

- sometimes do not ask or answer questions that may indicate their advanced ability because they do not want to appear 'different';

- do not often find set tasks challenging.

When teachers refer to pupils as gifted, they are often referring to actual performance perceived to be beyond that of age and stage peers. While Renzulli (1999) raises the question of definitions of the giftedness of individuals that sometimes cause teachers to get bogged down, he includes past accomplishments as part of the identification process. A focus on identification through provision rather than defining characteristics of gifted pupils is attractive to teachers who feel that identification and labelling is less important than ensuring that all pupils have access to high-quality learning and teaching opportunities.

Many secondary teachers find it relatively straightforward to identify pupils who are gifted in their subject area, though most will look for confirmation of their judgement through a combination of careful, sensitive observations in an atmosphere that encourages individual expression, together with some objective assessment, checklists, profiles or other criteria enabling them to build up detailed pictures of pupils upon which decisions about educational provision can be based.

STANDARDISED TESTS THAT COULD BE USED TO SUPPORT THE IDENTIFICATION OF GIFTED PUPILS

1. Hagues and Courtenay's (1993) *Verbal Reasoning* tests pupils' facility with language to measure wider reasoning ability. The results give information about pupils' abilities to acquire new concepts, information that may not be evident from their class work, an indication of how pupils assimilate new information and highlight their skills in verbal thinking beyond their formal literacy abilities.

2. Hagues and Smith's (1993) *Non-Verbal Reasoning* tests pupils' ability to recognise similarities, analogies and patterns in unfamiliar designs. The mental processes required to complete these tests demonstrate how pupils understand and assimilate new information, independent of language skills.

3. Heim et al.'s (1970) *The AH Series of Tests* offers assessments for measuring non-verbal and general reasoning and general intelligence. The perceptual reasoning assessment is ideal for pupils with reading difficulties or whose first language is not English. The 'general reasoning' assessment provides a single score as well as a detailed assessment with full individual profile.

4. Koshy and Casey's (2000) *Special Abilities Scales* offers a procedure for identifying high-ability pupils. The scales provide a structured basis for observational assessment which is accurate, consistent and effective: they generate a five-scale profile – learning, social leadership, creative thinking, self-determination and motivation. Designed for use by teachers and based on a checklist, these are easy to use and to score. The teacher's handbook gives extensive guidance on how to support able pupils, plus practical strategies for curriculum planning and organisation. The appendices contain photocopiable checklists and questionnaires.

5. Lohman et al.'s (2003) *Cognitive Abilities Test* measures three principal areas of reasoning – verbal, non-verbal and numerical – and spatial ability and can be used to build understanding of individual potential and learning. Six levels of testing are offered, enabling the assessment of pupils' verbal, non-verbal and quantitative reasoning abilities across the entire secondary phase.

6. Raven's (1938) *Progressive Matrices and Vocabulary Scales* offers a comprehensive verbal and non-verbal measure of ability. The test helps teachers to evaluate pupils' potential and identify those who are underachieving and those who need further challenges.

7. Smith and Lord's (2002) *Spatial Reasoning* assesses pupils' ability to manipulate shapes and patterns, and think in three dimensions. It helps

identify pupils with strong visual abilities who may find words a barrier to realising their potential in education. The test is word-free and non-culturally specific, so tests only spatial abilities, not linguistic knowledge, and is therefore ideal for assessing the abilities of students with English as an additional language or dyslexia. It identifies pupils with an aptitude for spatial subjects such as mathematics, physics, art and design and information and communication technology (ICT).

SOURCES OF IDENTIFICATION CHECKLISTS

1   Gross et al.'s (2001) *Gifted Students in Secondary Schools Differentiating the Curriculum* lists in Table1 (pp. 12–13) a number of characteristics of gifted students, together with an analysis of possible negative classroom behaviours, some classroom needs, and the resultant positive behaviours that may follow once the needs identified have been met. A very useful reference for the practitioner, as it could easily and quickly inform classroom practice.

2   Renzulli's (undated) *A Practical System for Identifying Gifted and Talented Students* revisits his 1986 characteristics of creative and productive individuals and summarises the major concepts and conclusions emanating from the work of theorists and researchers who have examined these, looking at general and specific ability, task commitment and creativity.

3   Goddard's (2001) *Gifted and Talented – Pack 1: Supporting Coordinators* contains several very useful checklists for the identification of gifted pupils:

- p. 6 How am I clever? For use with pupils for self-identification.

- pp. 7–13 Prompt sheets give lists of the characteristics of the seven different 'intelligences' identified by Gardner (1993) – linguistic, mathematical, musical, visual/spatial, kinaesthetic, interpersonal, intrapersonal.

- pp. 19–20 Identifying gifted and talented students – uses thinking skills in Bloom's Taxonomy.

- pp. 21–2 Characteristics of gifted and talented students are classified into categories – speech, learning, thinking, motivation, relationships, humour, arts, technical and morality.

- pp. 26–37 Subject-specific checklists identify giftedness across the whole secondary curriculum.

4   McMichael's (1998) *Identifying Able Pupils*
p. 19 A checklist covering behavioural and process characteristics, prepared for the gifted pupils' project in Montgomery's (1996) *Educating the Very Able*.

5   Hymer and Michel's (2002) *Gifted and Talented Learners*
pp. 21–48 Examples of a range of instruments for the identification of a gifted pupil using an identification-through-provision model.

6   Koshy and Casey's (2000) *Special Abilities Scales: Observational Assessment for Identifying Able and High-Potential Students* may be used to create profiles of individual learners.

7   Freeman's (1998) *Educating the Very Able: Current International Research* explores various methods that could support a teacher's identification of very able pupils:

- pp. 12–13 A research-based checklist for very able pupils.

- p. 15 Identifying disadvantaged highly-able children.

- p. 19 The sports approach: identification by provision.

- p. 23–4 Promoting self-regulation in learning.

8   George's (1997) *The Challenge of the Able Child*
    p. 35 A brief general identification checklist/rating scale, which teachers could use to construct a profile of a gifted pupil.

9   George's (1995) *Gifted Education Identification and Provision*

- p. 11 Mathematical ability checklist

- p. 12 Scientific ability, creative working, art ability – outlines items for inclusion in three checklists to identify giftedness in art, science or creativity.

- p. 14 Renzulli's rating scale – shows examples of characteristics of creativity, learning, leadership and motivation used by Renzulli and Hartman (1971).

10 Smith and Doherty's (1998) *Identifying Abilities in Individual Curricular Areas* is a report of a SNAP project looking at how abilities could be demonstrated in different areas of the curriculum:

- pp. 16–18 General checklists are grouped into three sub-groups dealing with information, linguistic skills and people skills.

- pp. 19–40 Subject-specific checklists – an analysis of the information required to identify subject ability.

- p. 41–2 Personal attributes – lists of positive and negative features.

- p. 43 Creativity – qualities considered to demonstrate creativity.

11 Eyre's (2002) *Effective Schooling for the Gifted and Talented*
    p. 15 Eight categories of information that might be sought.

12 Sutherland's (2002) *Identification of More Able Pupils*
    pp. 209–17 What schools would recognise as intelligent actions or behaviours.

13 Wallace's (2000) *Teaching the Very Able Child*
    pp. 27–53 Checklists of typical characteristics of high fliers, listing 32 indicators.

14 Teare's (1997) *Effective Provision for Able and Talented Children*
    pp. 29–32 Checklists of general characteristics and for mathematics, music and history.

📖 FURTHER READING

Hymer, B. and Michel, D. (2002) *Gifted and Talented Learners: Creating a Policy for Inclusion*. London: Futton

Montgomery, D. (1996) *Educating the Very Able*. London: Cassell

Smith, C.M. and Doherty, M. (1998) *Identifying Abilities in Individual Curricular Areas*. Glasgow: Scottish Network for Able Pupils

Sutherland, M. (2002) 'Identification of more able pupils: a pilot survey of Scottish schools', *Gifted Education International*, 18 (2): 209–17

Example of a Checklist of Gifted Behaviours

Subject Dept:

Pupil details:

Learning characteristics

☐ Has a history of early literacy and numeracy

☐ Has highly developed verbal skills and uses a sophisticated vocabulary

☐ Often finishes set work before classmates

☐ Follows complex instructions easily

☐ Works independently, using reference sources efficiently

☐ Good problem finding and solving skills

☐ Able to form and test hypotheses appropriately

☐ At ease in dealing with abstract ideas

☐ Studies subjects of interest in great depth

☐ Is very observant, able to find anomalies quickly

Behavioural characteristics

☐ Has an excellent concentration span

☐ Shows a vivid imagination with unusual ideas

☐ Often takes the initiative in intellectual and practical work

☐ Prefers to work alone, but may emerge as a leader in group work

☐ Shows originality and creativity

☐ Has a wide range of interests and hobbies

☐ Quickly gets bored with repetitive tasks

☐ Appears to have little in common with classmates

☐ Has an extraordinarily knowledge of obscure facts

☐ Has a good, sometimes bizarre, sense of humour

(P) Photocopiable: Supporting Gifted and Talented Pupils in the Secondary School
Paul Chapman Publishing 2006 © Moira Thomson

Chapter 3

Underachievement

This chapter looks at:

- Identification of underachievement
- Characteristics of underachievers
- Strategies for resolving the problems leading to underachievement
- Example of a checklist of underachievement
- Classroom strategy to prevent underachievement in reading
- Summer programme for gifted and talented pupils
- London Gifted & Talented
- The Real project

It is important to determine the reasons for underachievement in order to tackle it. While lack of appropriate educational provision and challenge contribute to underachievement, this may be linked to:

- disability or disadvantage;
- a desire to fit in with peers;
- low self-esteem.

Even well-qualified and competent teachers sometimes fail to challenge their most able pupils, for example giving 'extension' work that repeats already mastered material. These pupils are occupied but not challenged, and some of them appear to be quite content to work well below their capacity – underachievement that can be difficult to detect, since the pupils concerned are attaining the standards set for them. Gross (2004) finds it surprising that these gifted pupils do not rebel against inappropriate, undemanding educational provision more frequently, and points out that often they may deliberately underachieve – or 'dumb down' – in order to gain peer acceptance, making it even harder for the teacher to deal with.

IDENTIFICATION OF UNDERACHIEVEMENT

Poor interpersonal skills may play a part in underachievement by those pupils from poor socio-economic backgrounds or ethnic minorities or who have specific difficulties – whose abilities may not only be underestimated and undervalued but who are unable to find a way of demonstrating these in a school setting. These disadvantages often affect teachers' perceptions of pupils' capabilities, resulting in low expectations of their achievement that affect pupils' performance leading to a 'self-fulfilling prophecy' – if they are expected to perform in a certain way, or achieve at a certain level, then they probably will. Talents and skills can be ignored where they are not expected.

Underachievement is often identified through a pupil's demonstration of negative characteristics, and defined as a discrepancy between performance and other indications of ability or attainment that falls substantially below predicted levels. George (1997) categorises the causes and symptoms of underachievement as falling into three main areas:

- low self-esteem;
- academic avoidance behaviour;
- poor study habits.

These categories slot neatly into Gagné's differentiated model of giftedness and talents (2003b) where environmental, intrapersonal and chance catalysts are seen to impact on the developmental process of learning and prastising that is needed to transform potential into developed skills. While catalysts may be positive or negative, the combination of negative influences with an absence of positive input may result in underachievement.

Wallace (2000) looks at two categories of underachievement – the 'coasters' and the 'able but disaffected' – and explores positive and negative behaviours of underachievers, listing more than twice as many negatives as positives. It is common for some pupils with significant abilities who do not find school interesting and challenging to become alienated and disruptive, while others may limit themselves to the performance standards set for their age peers. Whether negative behaviour is a consequence of unsatisfying educational experiences or of low self-esteem, it can have a profound effect on achievement.

Negative indicators of underachievement fall into three categories:

- **Under-performing**, where performance is lower than intellectual potential and pupils produce little or no work though they show evidence of outstanding ability in a particular area. This group will include those who perform poorly in class due to boredom and lack of challenge and pupils from deprived socio-economic backgrounds who have not been identified as gifted because of low teacher expectations.
- **Divergent behaviour** by high potential pupils who may be aggressive, withdrawn or disruptive. Their actual ability may not be identified easily due to negative behaviour masking their potential.
- **Disadvantage**, where ability is masked by disability or disadvantaged backgrounds. Pupils may suffer from fear of failure, low self-esteem or pressure to conform and often require support to address difficulties linked to disadvantage and feelings of inferiority.

CHARACTERISTICS OF UNDERACHIEVERS

The characteristics of gifted underachievers often reflect the difficulties they encounter. Pupils from disadvantaged backgrounds may have low self-esteem and poorly developed study skills, resulting in failure to persevere at tasks and hostility to school and formal learning. Some pupils may be very able orally and mature in conversation but unable to write at length, with poor spelling and handwriting, leading to underestimation of their ability. Patterns of under-achievement often include:

- a very high IQ but low self-esteem;
- poor work habits and unfinished tasks;
- an apparent inability to concentrate;
- lack of effort in some work but an intense interest in one area;
- a skill deficit in one area or subject;
- a negative attitude towards self and age peers;
- demonstrations of emotional frustration;
- failure to respond to stimulation.

Because of continual failure in some areas, underachieving gifted pupils tend to exhibit either aggressive or withdrawn behaviour patterns alongside some characteristics of high ability. Features of the aggressive behaviour are:

- rejection of set tasks;
- lack of co-operation;
- disruption and alienation of others;

while withdrawn behaviour includes:

- lack of communication, preference for working alone;
- daydreaming, little set work undertaken;
- apparent lack of concern about attitude or behaviour.

Gifted underachievers can be hard to identify because they are both experienced and skilled at hiding their abilities. They may not have been identified by teachers, or others, as having abilities and learning needs that are in any way different from those of their age peers, and teachers may not have time to search for hidden abilities in unco-operative pupils.

To support the identification of underachieving gifted pupils, teachers might compile and use checklists (see 'Example of a checklist of underachieving behaviour' in this chapter). This should include general indicators of learning and behavioural characteristics as well as subject-specific items that could indicate high ability despite patterns of underachievement, for example:

Learning characteristics

- Very high IQ but hides abilities to gain peer acceptance.
- Poor work habits, lack of effort and unfinished work.
- Inability to concentrate but intense interest in one particular area.
- Rejection of set work and failure to respond to direct teacher input.
- Not motivated by results but fears failure, inhibiting attempts in new areas.
- Frustrated with inactivity and lack of challenge, may take on too many activities.
- Low self-esteem and negative attitude towards self and peers.

- Sets unrealistically high goals.
- Cynical attitude and emotional frustration.
- Stifled by lack of creative opportunities.
- Dominates discussion and has poor listening skills.
- Socially isolated but outwardly self-sufficient, rejected by others.
- Vulnerable to criticism, can blame things that go wrong on others.
- Uses humour inappropriately.

Behavioural characteristics

- Does not obey classroom rules and is confrontational.
- Attention seeking, ignores the needs of others.
- Prevents others from engaging with learning, disruptive.
- Can alienate classmates due to behaviour.
- Can appear bored, frustrated, stubborn and unco-operative.
- Can appear time-wasting or preoccupied.
- Impatient with slower thinkers.
- Tends to challenge and question indiscreetly.
- Lacks communication with classmates/teachers.
- Daydreams.
- Prefers to work alone and pursue own interests.
- Not much set work undertaken.
- Is confused when attempts at humour are not understood.
- Confused if thoughts and feelings are not taken seriously.
- Feels stifled by restrictions, works in own way and pace.

If pupils demonstrate a preponderance of items like these, together with indications of high subject ability, then it is probable that they are underachieving.

Of great concern to the teacher is the deliberate 'dumbing down' by gifted pupils. This may arise from a desire for age peer acceptance or because of a wish not to be different. The 'average' pupil can inflict considerable damage on the self-concept of a gifted classmate by providing false feedback about the true extent of his gifts (Gross, 1989). If this is accepted and internalised, a gifted pupil is likely to undervalue himself and his abilities. The resulting low self-esteem may impel the gifted pupil towards a disaffected group of less intellectual capacity, or in a rejection of academic pursuits in favour of performance related activities, perhaps in sport or music, where it is more acceptable to excel in the eyes of age peers.

Exposure to negative feedback and the need to protect themselves from rejection can result in some gifted individuals self-mocking to the extent of becoming 'class clowns' so that fragile self-concept is hidden and protected, or appearing cynical and dismissive of others in order to conceal low self-esteem. As a result of this protective camouflage, gifted pupils may increase their own alienation from the group and become even more isolated. They are often perceived by teachers and classmates as immature 'show-offs', resulting in intolerance from age peers and negative teacher attitudes. Gross (1998) exposes this, using case studies that illustrate the reasons why gifted pupils often feel that they have to conceal their true abilities and interests and the dilemmas they sometimes face as a result. Pupils in these studies have adopted alternative identities to reduce the risk of being rejected by their classmates.

The Templeton National Report on Acceleration (Colangelo et al., 2004) suggests that only slightly over half of the possible gifted learners in the United States are receiving education appropriate to their needs, and many researchers consider the gifted as the largest group of underachievers in education. If no one mentions their academic abilities, gifted pupils, who are often very perceptive, can be very unsure about the school's attitude to them. While teachers may have no hesitation in talking to gifted athletes or performers about their abilities, they are often reluctant to discuss academically gifted pupils' talents with them. Gifted pupils are often aware of this ambiguity, and this may cause them to doubt themselves or believe that their abilities are not valued, resulting in a lowering of self-esteem and achievement, and even to a disengagement from learning in the subject. If subject teachers make an effort to talk informally to gifted pupils about their specific abilities, they may feel that they have permission to be gifted and be less likely to conceal their abilities.

STRATEGIES FOR RESOLVING THE PROBLEMS LEADING TO UNDERACHIEVEMENT

Teachers might compile charts or tables (Gross et al., 2001) to trace negative behaviours resulting from characteristics of giftedness, and use these to explore possible classroom interventions. Underachievers may need intervention and support to change their behaviour (Freeman, 1998), and those who deliberately conceal their abilities may require changes in teachers' attitudes before they can emerge. Those who are confident in their abilities but choose not to comply with educational objectives may be largely impervious to any attempts to improve their attainment levels. These 'able but disaffected' pupils (Wallace, 2000: 32–4) range from the disillusioned to the apathetic, whose attitudes to learning and achievement may be equally difficult to affect.

Strategies to combat underachievement might include (Gross, 2001):

- Directed praise – to let the underachiever know that the teacher is aware that work could be better, and suggest improvements.

- Development of study and planning skills – many gifted underachievers rely on excellent memory and rapid reading/processing skills to coast through the curriculum. They may need structured help to develop strategies for dealing with increased challenge as they progress through the secondary school curriculum.

- Positive, not sarcastic or negative, comments – gifted underachievers are often overly sensitive to external criticism, and need to learn that this will not result in the withdrawal of support. Teachers can model the desired behaviour by being openly self-critical, admitting to mistakes and imperfections.

Gifted pupils are often bored and not engaged in school; they frequently underachieve, coasting through the curriculum, or feel alienated by the educational experiences on offer. Teachers need to look at the subject curriculum alongside the needs of their gifted pupils to determine where this is failing to provide the necessary challenge, then formulate curricular goals that address deficits in the core curriculum and develop a more effective, stimulating learning environment.

Example of a Checklist of Underachieving Behaviour

Subject Dept:

Pupil details:

Learning characteristics

☐ Is orally good but written work is poor – gap between expected and actual performance – may be reluctant to write at length because s/he cannot write as fast as s/he thinks

☐ Is apparently bored, may appear to be absorbed in a private world

☐ Often abandons set work before finishing, having mastered content/process

☐ Can follow complex instructions easily, but may prefer to do things differently

☐ Works independently, but finds many reference sources superficial

☐ Good problem finding skills, but reluctant to solve these once identified

☐ Inventive in response to open-ended questions, able to form but not test hypotheses

☐ At ease in dealing with abstract ideas

☐ Shows a vivid imagination with unusual ideas

☐ Is very observant, perhaps argumentative, able to ask provocative questions

Behavioural characteristics

☐ Has a poor concentration span but is creative and persevering when motivated

☐ May be emotionally unstable – feelings of inferiority but outwardly self-sufficient

☐ Often restless and inattentive, lacks task commitment

☐ Prefers to work alone, rarely co-operates in group work

☐ Shows originality and creativity but quickly gets bored with repetitive tasks

☐ Has a narrow range of interests and hobbies with extraordinary knowledge of obscure facts

☐ Appears to have little in common with classmates, being tactless and impatient with slower minds

☐ Has a quirky, sometimes adult, sense of humour

CASE STUDY

Classroom strategy to prevent underachievement in reading

Aspect of underachievement: reading for information is much poorer than standardised testing indicates.

Identification:

- Checklists are completed by observation of pupils in associated primary schools prior to transfer to secondary.
- Detailed information about ability and achievement in subject areas is passed to secondary departments by the primary class teacher.
- Standardised tests of reading are done as part of the transition process.
- Other measures of reading ability such as off-level testing are available to secondary school staff.

English Department: differentiation strategies designed to prevent underachievement in reading for information.

Philosophical Enquiry programmes (COPE) already in place in many primary schools are developed alongside Independent Thinking and Critical Skills programmes in order to help motivate those first-year secondary pupils who already demonstrate highly-developed reading skills.

When the class works with the English teacher on reading activities, this group works with a designated member of the senior management team on activities designed to enable them to:

- develop understanding of complex text using newspaper and magazine articles and other materials selected by pupils;
- demonstrate developing critical skills and attitudes;
- consider the context of texts including social, economic and philosophical influences on the writers.

Progress is monitored using higher-level close reading passages and the programme evaluated in discussion with the senior managers involved.

CASE STUDY

Summer programme for gifted and talented pupils

There are lots of summer programmes to promote innovation and diversity in out of school hours learning, using grants from The National Lottery's New Opportunities Fund. One such programme run by the City of Edinburgh Council is offered free of charge to gifted pupils who have just completed their first year at secondary school.

The decision to offer the programme to pupils at this stage of secondary education was based on research which indicated that many gifted pupils begin to underachieve during the second year of secondary school. The programme was specifically targeted at these pupils in an attempt to prevent this, and characteristics of underachievers were included in checklists issued to schools to help inform their nomination procedures.

CONTINUED

The programme aimed to consolidate existing secondary school gifted education provision by offering opportunities to explore new activities, and to challenge and motivate pupils in drama, art, philosophy, environmental science and technology.

Pupils were nominated by their schools, based on selection criteria specified by course tutors. These criteria were designed to help schools identify pupils who have already shown high ability and who are enthusiastic, imaginative, creative, able to work independently, and at risk of underachievement. Schools responded enthusiastically to the nomination process and the available places could have been filled several times over. Some pupils, evaluating their experiences, said that nomination for the programme improved their confidence and raised self-esteem.

Those pupils selected for the programme worked for a week with a team of enthusiastic teachers who give up part of their summer holiday to deliver this intensive tuition. Pupils were also able to experience fencing with specialist instructors. At the end of the week a morning of presentations and exhibitions gave everyone the chance to show their considerable achievements to parents and guests. All pupils who have participated in the programme agreed that they shared a really good experience.

Credit for the success of the programme goes to schools who identify pupils, to the tutors, who work hard to provide challenging and stimulating activities, and particularly to the pupils themselves, whose enthusiasm and hard work has been an inspiration to everyone involved. It is worth noting the voluntary return of some pupils in later years as 'helpers'. Without exception, the participants, their parents and their teachers agreed that the summer programme was a positive experience for all concerned, and this has been carried back enthusiastically to their schools, ensuring continued support of the programme.

CASE STUDY

London Gifted & Talented (http://www.londongt.org)

The gifted and talented education arm of the London Challenge

London Gifted & Talented is a public-private consortium and has been operating since January 2004 and is intended to provide a potential model of cross-authority collaboration at a regional level. This partnership provides an opportunity for talented people to work together to improve provision for gifted and talented pupils, with a particular focus on tackling disadvantage and underachievement. In the long term, it is hoped to extend this model to other areas of England.

The main aims of London Gifted & Talented are to:

- raise motivation and performance of gifted and talented pupils;
- improve professional practice re gifted and talented in London schools;
- build integrated provision in partnership with key educational stakeholders;
- create models of effective practice that can be extended into other educational arenas;
- cascade key skills and knowledge through schools and the wider community;
- act as the London Regional Gateway for the National Academy for Gifted & Talented Youth.

CONTINUED

Pupils and teachers are connected with specialists and experts in leading academic, cultural and sporting institutions through specially created learning programmes that combine live events, such as master classes or workshops and cutting edge e-learning, with a range of activities to ensure longer-term impact.

With key partners, London Grid for Learning, Digitalbrain and Mouchel Parkman, six 'thematic networks' have been developed including 'Raising the Achievement of African-Caribbean Pupils', 'Working with Parents' and 'Transition between Phases'.

CASE STUDY

The Real project (http://www.intoreal.com)

Real at the Lighthouse was a part of a much larger project undertaken by Scottish Enterprise Glasgow. The aim of this project was to help young people who had become disengaged from the learning process to develop practical tools and positive approaches to creativity. Individual goals and popular culture provided the 'hook' to engage them in learning, helping to equip them with the kind of competencies and skills needed for employment. Pupils did not have to be in school to access the activities in the programme; they could go on-line from anywhere in the city, including public libraries.

Learning Bites

The Learning Bites programme was a Web-based education initiative, intended to explore and deliver innovative approaches to on-line learning, particularly in fields where information technology is making an impact. These accessible 'bites' of on-line learning lasted between 10 minutes and 1 hour.

Learning Cafés

Learning Cafés were one-off events at The Lighthouse which provided guidance for the Learning Bites programme and explored specific areas within the creative industries, including Internet broadcasting, music production and filmmaking.

Learning Cards

Learning Cards complemented the activities undertaken during the Learning Bites, Learning Cafés and related workshops. These cards reinforced all information discussed during these events and listed useful telephone numbers, websites and details of local courses.

Workshops

Disengaged youngsters worked with professionals:

- *Radio Magnetic* provided training on setting up Internet radio stations, as well as website design, marketing and broadcast programme training.
- *Sasequatch Productions* explored all aspects of the music industry, featuring sound and visual training and other disciplines including DJing/VJing techniques.

CONTINUED

Learning journals

Participants in the workshops, cafés and other learning events were encouraged to record their activities, thoughts and achievements in their own personal creative journal. This allowed them to reflect on past activities and to plan next steps, if any, in their education.

The main objective was to encourage able, disengaged teenagers to re-enter education in a way that they might find relevant to their interests. Few were expected to re-engage with the secondary schools they had rejected (or been rejected by), but links to suitable courses in colleges of further education were encouraged – and taken up.

📖 FURTHER READING

Gross, M.U.M. (1998) 'The "Me" behind the mask: intellectually gifted students and the search for identity', *Roeper Review, A Journal on Gifted Education*, 20 (3)

Moon, S.M. (2003) 'Personal talent', *High Ability Studies*, 14 (1): 5–21

Moon, S.M. (ed.) (2004) *Social/Emotional Issues, Underachievement, and Counseling of Gifted and Talented Students*. Thousand Oaks, CA: Corwin Press.

USEFUL WEBSITES

http://www.jnpartnership.co.uk/main.php/232/362/51
http://www.standards.dfes.gov.uk/thinkingskills/guidance
http://www.independentthinking.co.uk
http://www.criticalskills.co.uk/index.html
http://www.sapere.org.uk/
http://www.p4c.org.nz/
http://www.londongt.org/homepage/index.php
http://www.londongt.org/homepage/index.php

Chapter 4

Dual Exceptionality

This chapter looks at:

- What is meant by dual exceptionality
- Giftedness and:
  - physical/sensory impairment
  - developmental disorders, e.g
    - autism
    - dyslexia
- Successful people who have physical or sensory impairments
- Successful dyslexics

Dual exceptionality is the combination of giftedness with a disability or specific difficulty that may affect learning. Social and behavioural difficulties fall into this category only as issues that may be part of another condition affecting learning.

In a climate of increasingly inclusive educational provision, many teachers are already aware that some types of learning difficulties are not uncommon among the most highly gifted, and have accepted that to meet the learning needs of their most gifted pupils effectively, they must be ready to deal with learning difficulties resulting from conditions such as autism and dyslexia.

Research has indicated that there are many more gifted children who have special educational needs than had been thought; one-third of children identified as gifted by Silverman (1989) also had a learning difficulty. While many difficulties are overt and easily identified, a significant number are hidden and may prevent the revelation of characteristics of giftedness, resulting in pupils being considered 'average' by teachers (Montgomery, 2003). In order to identify fully the potential abilities of this group of pupils, teachers need to explore the hidden effects of disability and provide an appropriate and challenging curriculum that will enable all pupils' gifts to emerge.

GIFTEDNESS AND PHYSICAL IMPAIRMENT

There are problems linked to physical impairment that may mask ability in secondary-age pupils. The structure of the school day may adversely affect a pupil who has mobility difficulties and is placed at a disadvantage compared to age peers because of the extra effort required just to move around the building, resulting in low energy levels and increasing fatigue, making it difficult to keep up with the demands of the curriculum. Many teachers recognise this and provide support for these pupils, but few understand the full implications of the impact of exhaustion on learning and provide strategies that, while enabling pupils to follow a full mainstream curriculum, do so by turning them into non-participating observers, possibly preventing them from demonstrating ability. A pupil with a condition affecting hands and wrists will be unable to produce written work to the same extent as classmates, even with the support of a laptop computer, leading to an inability to reveal actual attainment through writing. This may be taken by subject teachers to indicate impaired performance rather than the inability to hold a pen or use a keyboard, not because they do not understand the implications of the physical condition but because they are unable to comprehend the cumulative effects of the demands of the curriculum on the individual.

Cerebral palsy is a neurological condition resulting in a disorder of movement or posture. In milder cases, pupils may limp or have limited use of arms, while more severe instances confine pupils to wheelchairs and impair speech. While cognitive ability is not affected, a pupil's opportunities to demonstrate this are restricted, resulting in a lack of appropriate challenge in some subjects and leading eventually to underachievement. The secondary school may offer therapy, specialised technology and adult help to support inclusion, but this will not prevent underachievement unless the pupil's learning and communication needs are dealt with separately.

The term 'physical impairment' is also used to describe a range of less obvious conditions which may interfere with an individual pupil's ability to learn in the same way and at the same rate as age peers, for example, diabetes or epilepsy.

GIFTEDNESS AND SENSORY IMPAIRMENT

Visual impairment may affect a pupil's ability to imitate social behaviour or understand non-verbal cues and may result in developmental delays in spatial awareness. Because visually impaired pupils may need additional help involving special equipment and curriculum modifications which emphasise listening skills and communication, most subject teachers focus on adapting their subject delivery in order to avoid placing pupils at a disadvantage. While the range of ability in visually impaired pupils will reflect that of the general population, difficulties created by a deficit in visual processing may conceal characteristics of giftedness. All gifted learners need to proceed through the developmental process of learning and practice to transform innate gifts into developed skills, and educational provision that focuses on compensating for visual deficits may fail to provide opportunities for this, resulting in a lack of challenge and underachievement. Gifted pupils with visual impairments should be included in existing programmes that are modified only to accommodate visual problems (Starr, 2003). Teachers need to consider how to build on the strengths of visually impaired pupils, often in the auditory–verbal range, in order to support fragile self-esteem and the development of abilities that may otherwise remain hidden.

While pupils who are hearing impaired find it much more difficult than age peers to learn vocabulary, grammar, idiomatic expressions and other aspects of verbal communication, hearing loss does not affect a pupil's intellectual capacity or ability to learn, so, as with visually-impaired pupils, difficulties linked to deafness and teachers' tendency to focus on resolving these may prevent the identification of giftedness (Winstanley, 2003).

Teachers sometimes identify gifted pupils who have a physical or sensory impairment as being of average ability, despite evidence of the extraordinary efforts they put into some activities and their levels of attainment in some subjects. Consideration should be given to the extraordinary achievements of gifted individuals who are known to have physical or sensory impairments, not only to provide role models for pupils, but also to remind teachers of the hidden potential that may be present in all pupils.

GIFTEDNESS AND DEVELOPMENTAL DISORDERS

There is a cluster of developmental disorders which includes dyslexia, dyspraxia, autism, ADHD and language disorders. Pupils who have these difficulties are likely to develop skills at a different rate, or in a different way from their classmates. Language plays a major role in all school subjects, being the medium by which information is communicated. At secondary school, mastery of language is assumed and emphasis is placed on written skills. As pupils progress through the secondary curriculum, complex use of language is expected, including an increased, subject-specific vocabulary, more advanced sentence structure, and the use of different registers for different situations. Language disorders in pupils at secondary school can lead to feelings of failure, low self-esteem and poor academic and social success.

GIFTEDNESS AND AUTISM

The autistic 'savant' is an individual who demonstrates exceptional ability in one area, while being considerably impaired in social interaction and language, and may be a genius of a different kind (Hendrickson, 2001). While we never doubt the gifts that go with able brains, we are much less willing to credit disabled brains with extraordinary talents that unimpaired brains cannot easily match. Savant abilities are associated with hyper-sensitivity linked to the five primary senses, as well as obsessive behaviour and selective attention. Obsession with sound–hearing becomes a musical activity; obsession with the visuo–spatial sense can be expressed through drawing, chess and mathematics;

while a tactile–spatial obsession can be transferred to sculpture. No autistic savants have (yet) appeared in creative literature, philosophy or physics – where creativity and imagination are essential elements.

Asperger's syndrome differs from high-functioning autism through early acquisition of speech, and by the presence of some degree of motor impairment. Those who have Asperger's lack social or emotional reciprocity, show a preoccupation with interests that goes beyond normal intensity, have an uneven profile of abilities with remarkable long-term memory, exceptional concentration when engaged in their special interest, and an original method of problem solving. Gifted pupils also exhibit these characteristics, sometimes placing them at risk of being mistakenly identified as having Asperger's syndrome because their atypical social interactions or unusual methods of commenting and joking is misinterpreted. Both groups may show motor clumsiness, lack motivation and attention for activities that engage age peers, exhibit social withdrawal, experience teasing by peers and have difficulty relating to others in an age-appropriate manner, increasing the possibility of confusion. However, gifted pupils will benefit from interventions like the opportunity to interact with appropriate peers, while Asperger's pupils do not.

A significant number of Asperger's pupils are of high ability (Montgomery, 2003) and show many of the characteristics of giftedness, so they are often considered to be gifted eccentrics rather than being on the autistic spectrum. The presence of giftedness not only masks Asperger's but also goes some way towards alleviating the depression that is often part of this syndrome (Gallagher and Gallagher, 2001). However, behavioural issues linked to Asperger's often conceal pupils' considerable abilities; they may not consider that school routines and rules apply to them, and teachers often find this particularly difficult to deal with. Asperger's behaviour can be ritualised, rigid and difficult to change, resulting in conflict with teachers and classmates (Montgomery, 2003), sometimes leading to exclusion from school without high ability being noticed because of the masking effect of difficult behaviour.

Those pupils who have language disorders exhibit similarities to Asperger's with social interaction difficulties, but their behaviour tends to be withdrawn rather than disruptive. Giftedness in these pupils is often in the visual and performance areas, where the deficit in language processing has lower impact. Although not as obsessive as those on the autistic spectrum, they can become absorbed in the study of a single subject to the exclusion of all else, often ingeniously linking unrelated topics to their area of special interest.

GIFTEDNESS AND DYSLEXIA

Although the symptoms of dyslexia were first recognised many years ago, there is still no universal agreement on classifying the various manifestations of this. Doctors and researchers may focus on differences in genetics and brain organisation and function, while psychologists often focus on dysfunctions in perception, processing, memory and attention, while teachers are more concerned with specific areas of academic difficulties and the impact of the dyslexia on pupils' learning and attainment.

Dyslexia describes a different kind of mind, often gifted and productive, that learns differently. Though most dyslexic pupils experience difficulties linked to processing written language, they are often bright, creative and talented individuals. Many have unusual talent in areas that require visual, spatial and motor integration such as art, athletics, architecture, graphics, mechanics or engineering, and may show highly developed social skills as well as gifts in technology, science, and mathematics. The usual educational emphasis on dyslexic pupils' weaknesses can adversely impact on self-esteem. Teachers often excel at designing programmes to compensate for deficits in literacy or memory, but can be less proficient in providing challenge and support in areas of giftedness. There is a need to balance remediation with a rich and stimulating curriculum that identifies and nurtures the strengths and gifts of dyslexic pupils.

There is a growing popular view that individuals with dyslexia have compensatory visual–spatial talents that allow them to excel in spatial activities such as computer graphics. There is a high incidence of individuals with dyslexia in professions requiring spatial abilities, professions such as art, engineering or architecture (West, 1997, 1999). The gifts and talents of highly successful dyslexics may be more noticeable because of the contrast between exceptional capabilities and specific disabilities, and inconsistencies between high intelligence and ability and unexpectedly poor reading and writing skills. Many teacher interventions focus on obvious problems to be corrected, rather than hidden potential to be identified and developed.

Studies show that highly successful dyslexic individuals achieve through following substantial gifts, not by focusing on difficulties. It is becoming clear that we need to find ways of changing the traditional educational focus from compensation for the deficits of dyslexic pupils to celebration of their differences, and we must find ways to minimize the impact of these in assessments of attainment. The more we are able to do this, the more likely we will be to provide an appropriately challenging curriculum for dyslexics and others whose disabilities conceal their abilities.

CASE STUDY

Successful people who have physical or sensory impairments

Teachers might find a study of highly successful individuals who have a physical or sensory impairment a useful guide to the possibilities of giftedness in their pupils, whose talents are masked either by their disability or by the measures put in place to minimise the effect of this on inclusion in mainstream school. The examples of high attainment in various areas listed below might also serve as appropriate role models for disabled pupils; after all, while a mobility-impaired pupil might admire the accomplishments of talented able-bodied individuals, only the success of similarly impaired individuals could offer role models whose accomplishments might be aspired to or mirrored.

Visually impaired

Musicians, **José Feliciano** and **Stevie Wonder**, who were born blind, have been major figures within the US music scene over the last 40 years. **Ray Charles** has been described by many writers as 'a genius' and the 'father of soul music'. He was slowly blinded by glaucoma until, at the age of six, he had lost his sight completely.

Hearing impaired

Linking the hearing impaired with music may seem unusual, until one remembers **Ludwig van Beethoven**, whose musical genius – and progressive deafness – are well documented.

Percussionist **Evelyn Glennie's** career, like that of Beethoven's, is considered by many to be an impossibility. She has said: *'There are only three possible explanations: I am not a musician, I'm not deaf, or the general understanding of the categories of "Deaf" or "Music" must be incorrect.'* Although she is profoundly deaf, she prefers not to dwell on this: *'If you want to know about deafness, you should interview an audiologist. My specialty is music.'*

Physically impaired

Stephen Hawking's achievements are awe-inspiring, but he wrote scientific papers by dictating to a secretary and gave seminars through an interpreter. *'I have had motor neurone disease for practically all my adult life. Yet it has not prevented me from being successful in my work.'*

Britain's greatest ever paralympic athlete, **Tanni Grey-Thompson**, has competed in five Paralympic Games, achieving 11 gold, 4 silver and 1 bronze medals over 16 years, making her one of the most gifted and courageous sportswomen of her generation. The secret of her success is her motivation: *'For me it's not about pretending I don't have a disability. I'm just a very competitive person. I love finishing a hard session and not being sure if I'm going to be sick or not.'*

Successful dyslexics

Why do some dyslexics succeed so dramatically while others struggle to survive, never seeming to realise their potential? Davis (1994) will tell you that dyslexia is a gift. But there are few dyslexic people who have struggled with its effects when they were at school who would agree completely with this view. However, there is no doubt that some dyslexic people who are visual, multi-dimensional thinkers are gifted in certain areas, even if they never did succeed educationally. Being intuitive and highly creative, they are often much better at hands-on learning, though it may be difficult for them to understand letters, numbers, symbols and written words. At school, the impact of dyslexia often makes it difficult for teachers to identify giftedness.

Stories of those who have already succeeded may be the best guides to promote understanding of how to create success where there is so often failure. The giftedness of many dyslexics seems to be strong in art, architecture, engineering, computing and performance arts as well as entrepreneurial business. These are areas where achievement is measured by demonstrated success, often

CONTINUED

more highly valued in society than traditional academic skills. The following personal comments and case histories may offer new insight into dyslexia and giftedness.

Winston Churchill lacked self-esteem when young and was considerably discouraged by his school days. *'It was not pleasant to feel oneself so completely outclassed and left behind at the beginning of the race.'*

Erin Brockovich hid her dyslexia for a long time, as she felt recognition of the disability would 'label' her. She identified persistence and determination as components to her success. *'People called me stupid – I knew that I could learn, but I just couldn't learn the way that society wanted to teach me. There are no set answers, just be who you are.'*

Richard Branson is a well-known media figure and hot-air balloonist who has tried several times to circle the globe, best known as the operator of over 150 businesses – airlines, railways, recording companies and investment services. As a dyslexic, he reported: *'I have a little trouble telling left from right. That's why I paint my parachute release bright red, because I accidentally pulled it once instead of the rip cord and the chute came off.'* School wasn't just a challenge for him, it was a nightmare. His dyslexia embarrassed him and he didn't pass the entrance exams for university. For him, exams did not identify the ambition that drove him to succeed and failed to identify his most important gift: the ability to interact with people.

Physicist **Albert Einstein** had severe reading, writing and maths difficulties. He could figure out the connections of the universe, but needed help from a mathematician to formulate his theories. He had a blackboard in his study, where multiplication tables were written; in common with many dyslexics, he never did manage to learn them. His teachers reported that he was *'mentally slow',* he was *'unsociable', 'adrift forever in his foolish dreams'.*

Film director **Guy Ritchie** is very dyslexic and his abilities were completely masked by this at school. Although he couldn't write he had a lot to say, and he has gone on to forge a successful career in the film world.

Successful actress **Susan Hampshire** has spent many years publicising the negative effects of dyslexia and promoting strategies for overcoming them, inspiring others like actor **Orlando Bloom** who struggled in many subjects at school because of his dyslexia. He did well in the arts and enjoyed pottery, photography and sculpture as well as performing in school plays, eventually going on to drama college and a successful career as an actor.

David Bailey, photographer: *'At school, I was put in the class for the stupid. I have yet to write a letter and still write figures the wrong way round.'* These difficulties did not prevent Bailey from becoming one of the world's most successful photographers. He considers that visual people are luckier than verbal people because they are not limited by their vocabulary.

Taliesin-trained architect and artist **Bennett Strahan** is dyslexic and paints – and even sees – backwards. As a boy, he read by holding books up to mirrors. He was treated as borderline retarded, until his artistic gift became clear. Despite his early difficulties, he now sees his dyslexia in a different light: *'I think it has probably helped me more than any single thing I can think of,'* he says. *'Three-dimensional thinking was what was created by the dyslexia problem. I could design these things in my head.'*

Tommy Hilfiger, fashion designer, often acted as the 'class clown' in an attempt to hide his dyslexia from his classmates. *'I performed poorly at school,* *when I attended, that is, and was perceived as stupid because of my dyslexia. I still have trouble reading. I have to concentrate very hard at going left to right, left to right; otherwise my eye just wanders to the bottom of the page.'*

Irish poet **W.B. Yeats** was dyslexic and also had negative educational experiences. *'My father was an angry and impatient teacher and flung the reading book at my head'.* Yeats produced highly idiosyncratic versions of words all his life despite his highly acclaimed writing. He founded the Irish Academy of Letters, and reformed the Irish Literary Society, and then the National Literary Society in Dublin to promote the New Irish Library.

Novelist **Agatha Christie** was always considered to be the 'slow one' in the family. *'Writing and spelling were always terribly difficult for me. My letters were without originality. I was . . . an extraordinarily bad speller and have remained so until this day.'*

A number of successful people who struggled at school discovered their dyslexia when they took their children to be tested. **Cher**, actress and musician, had successful strategies in place to cope with her dyslexic difficulties but had no idea that these were due to dyslexia until she took her daughter to be tested. *'I never read in school. I had to learn by listening. My reports said I was not living up to my potential. I got really bad grades. I just quit.'*

Sir Jackie Stewart, former world champion racing driver, Olympic hopeful in shooting and successful businessman thought he *'was just stupid, dumb or thick'* because he couldn't read or spell like other people. His dyslexia was not diagnosed until he was 42, when he took his sons to be tested. Sir Jackie, now president of Dyslexia Scotland, insists that *'Early diagnosis is the biggest and most important thing you can get to help a young person'.*

Total dedication and determination to succeed at something has led to the highest achievement in several sporting areas. Winner of five consecutive Olympic gold medals for rowing, **Sir Steven Redgrave** struggled at school due to his dyslexia. His difficulties in the classroom troubled him but he was determined to prove that he could be good at something – he certainly succeeded in that. Basketball great **Magic Johnson** was tired of being laughed at because of his dyslexia and he wanted to show everybody that he could do better, motivating him to become one of the world's greatest basketball players.

American paleontologist **Dr John R. Horner** is a highly-talented and innovative dyslexic working in science. He has an honorary doctorate and supervises Ph.D. candidates, but he never completed an undergraduate degree or any graduate work. He 'flunked out' of the University of Montana six times, but his brilliant synthesis of evidence forced paleontologists to revise their ideas about dinosaur behaviour, physiology and evolution. In spite of his persistent academic failures, he came eventually to be acknowledged as one who has transformed some of the fundamental thinking in his field. *'Nobody knew what dyslexia was ... everybody thought you were lazy or stupid or both. I like to find things that nobody else has found, like a dinosaur egg that has an embryo inside. There are 36 of them in the world, and I found 35.'*

In common with many other gifted dyslexics, Horner had extraordinary difficulties with things that are largely peripheral to his discipline – reading, writing/spelling, exams – resulting in perceived underachievement in school. But he proved to be unusually gifted in those things at the heart of his discipline: being unusually observant while searching for fossil bones; able to interpret patterns from evidence; developing innovative and persuasive arguments based on looking at raw data in a very different way.

📖 FURTHER READING

Gray-Thompson, T. (2002) *Seize the Day: My Autobiography*. London: Coronet Books

Miles, T. R., Westcombe, J. and Snowling, M. (eds) (2001) Music and Dyslexia: *Opening Doors*. London: Whurr.

Webb, J.T., Amend, E.R., Webb, N.E., Goerss, J., Beljan, P. and Olenchak, F.R. (eds) (2005) *Misdiagnosis and Dual Diagnoses of Gifted Children and Adults: ADHD, Bipolar, OCD, Asperger's, Depression, and Other Disorders*. Scottsdale, AZ: Great Potential Press.

West, T. G. (1997) *In the Mind's Eye*. New York: Promethius.

USEFUL WEBSITES

1   Evelyn Glennie website: Keynote speech at a seminar for teachers of 'Special Education Needs' students http://www.evelyn.co.uk/disabled.htm: Essay on Deafness http://www.evelyn. co.uk/hearing.htm

2   Stephen Hawking: Disability – *My Experience with ALS* http://www.hawking.org.uk/text/disable/disable.html

3   The Jurassics Foundation, Dr John R. Horner – Biographical details retrieved on 18 April 2005 from http://www.magtech.ab.ca/jurassic/horner.htm

Chapter 5

Policy and Provision

This chapter looks at:

- Policies
- Provision
- Local strategies
- Individual school strategies
- Inclusive provision
- School organisational strategies
- School policy framework for gifted education
- Provision for gifted and talented pupils at secondary school
- Support for gifted and talented pupils at secondary school
- Implementing policies
- Timeline of UK initiatives in gifted education

POLICIES

In many countries initiatives to provide appropriate education for gifted pupils exist (Eyre, 2004), but these may not be available to all pupils, or are perhaps restricted to activities that are not part of the school curriculum. Development of a gifted education policy is essential to ensure that pupils have opportunities to develop their abilities and skills to become the future intellectual, social, economic and cultural leaders.

Although specific provision for gifted pupils is rarely defined by education policy, different countries have taken various approaches over the years ranging from selective schools providing academic or vocational curricula, common in some European countries, to completely inclusive provision where gifted pupils are taught entirely in mixed ability classrooms. Some countries such as New Zealand (Riley et al., 2004) and England (Eyre, 2004) have well-developed national policies, while others, like Scotland, have introduced a national advisory body to provide advice for teachers, parents and pupils, and training for individuals and groups (Smith, C.M. et al., 2003). Many countries have produced detailed government reports and issued guidance based on these for local/state authorities to follow in devising and updating their own policies and making provision for implementing these.

PROVISION

Educational provision is usually organised on three main levels: government policy, local provision within a policy framework, and individual school-based initiatives and strategies. Government policies and initiatives may identify their gifted and talented population in terms of percentages; for example, in England a relative population of 10 per cent of pupils in a school may be identified as gifted or talented (Dracup, 2004). In some countries, making separate provision for pupils of high ability is seen as elitism and preferential treatment, while in others it is thought that inclusive schooling does not meet the learning needs of gifted and talented pupils and may result in underachievement, social or economic disadvantage.

Gifted education may be seen as additional to the main educational system, but in order to make appropriate provision for all pupils and address concerns about underachievement, arrangements to meet the needs of those who are gifted and talented must be integrated into mainstream provision.

LOCAL STRATEGIES

On a local level, provision usually fits into the framework set out in government policy and defines arrangements made to meet the needs of those gifted and talented pupils for whom local authorities have responsibility. This may include several strategies:

- developing a local policy for schools to implement or providing schools with a framework to devise their own policies;
- offering support and advice to schools for gifted educational provision;
- providing schools with access to specialist advice;
- arranging for specialist activities, which may not be cost-effective for a single school to provide, to be available to all schools in the area, for example, master classes, holiday programmes;
- encouraging schools to develop after-school clubs and enrichment activities;
- supporting schools by disseminating details of best practice;
- providing training for school staff in the identification of and provision for gifted pupils;
- providing subject-specific guidance for teachers so that they may deliver effectively challenging curricula to gifted and talented pupils;
- monitoring and evaluating gifted educational provision in schools.

INDIVIDUAL SCHOOL STRATEGIES

At the secondary school level, provision will focus on in-school provision designed to implement national and local policies. A school policy for the support of gifted pupils should be based on guidance from education authorities and designed to address arrangements for the identification of gifted pupils and details of how the school intends to make appropriate provision for them. These arrangements may be innovative but usually build on existing practice within the school, including aims linked to raising attainment, and indicate how an evaluation of the process and outcomes will take place.

Strategies that individual schools may use to support gifted pupils include:

- school policy for gifted and talented pupils that reflects practice;
- a designated co-ordinator responsible for gifted pupils;
- opportunities for staff development;
- monitoring the progress and attainment of gifted and talented pupils.

INCLUSIVE PROVISION

When exploring reasons why schools were not meeting the needs of their most able pupils, Eyre (1997) found that 'Something in the region of 80 per cent of that which constitutes good provision for able pupils can be found in any good school.'

Some educators consider the inclusion of gifted pupils in mainstream classrooms merely cost-effective, but others, aware of issues of underachievement and disadvantage, may promote inclusive education as the best way to meet the needs of all pupils effectively. If provision for the education of gifted pupils is integrated into overall provision, an appropriate learning environment and enriched curriculum will give previously unrecognised gifted pupils opportunities to demonstrate their abilities and develop their talents. Care should be taken that the provision of inclusive education does not lead to a focus on the learning needs of the less able in the belief that gifted pupils will reach their potential without additional support.

SCHOOL ORGANISATIONAL STRATEGIES

Many believe that it is possible to deliver much of the curriculum to gifted pupils in mixed ability classes – the inclusion agenda. Some secondary schools place pupils in separate sets for mathematics, science and modern languages, since these subjects are usually taught sequentially, requiring mastery of and building upon developed skills before it is possible for pupils to progress through the curriculum. If a secondary school adopts a mixed ability grouping arrangement for these subjects, then it must have strategies in place to ensure that gifted pupils are not penalised by the pace of the class being aimed at the slower pupils.

Whatever grouping arrangements schools employ, they should be in the best interests of all pupils concerned. Examples of grouping arrangements are:

- *Streaming*, where pupils are grouped according to general ability, often measured by scores on standardised tests of intelligence, reading and mathematics, does not take account of differing developmental rates of pupils, nor of abilities in other aspects of the curriculum.

- *Setting*, where pupils are grouped according to ability in a subject, allows pupils who are good at individual subjects to experience a more appropriately challenging curriculum, but, while effective, this strategy is expensive and difficult to timetable in a secondary school, so is often limited to a few subjects, making provision for gifted pupils uneven.

- *Mixed-ability*, where gifted pupils are taught in the same class as the least able, could involve a very wide ability range and developmental gap between pupils. It is an inclusive approach requiring well-differentiated teaching to meet a diversity of abilities in one class.

- *Broad-banding*, where pupils are loosely grouped according to attainment and progress through the curriculum at different rates, has the advantage of reducing the developmental gap in a mixed-ability class, and makes the teacher's task of providing appropriate differentiation of the curriculum more manageable.

- *Vertical grouping*, where pupils are taught in mixed-age groups, can be very effective, enabling pupils of similar ability to be taught together, though it may be difficult to timetable in a secondary school, where different year groups attend different subject classes at different times, but exceptional arrangements could be put in place when the needs of an individual pupil require a more advanced subject curriculum.

- *Fast-tracking*, where an accelerated path is taken through a particular subject, by individuals or groups of pupils, who may take qualifications ahead of their year group, often involving curriculum compacting where only new subject content is taught to gifted pupils.

- *Extraction*, where gifted pupils leave the normal class for 'special' experiences and courses. Enrichment activities are an accepted way of making effective provision for gifted pupils, and this is a common approach in many secondary schools, but if these are provided only for the gifted, this system could be seen as elitist and lead to dissatisfaction across the school community.

- *Extra-curricular activities and clubs* are usually voluntary and attract those with a particular interest or ability in a subject. Many of these groups have a focus that is not offered in the school curriculum, while others provide opportunities for more in-depth explorations of favourite subjects and some, like drama groups, offer additional performance opportunities.

Whatever grouping organisation is in place in their schools, teachers need to employ diverse and flexible teaching and learning strategies that meet the needs of distinct pupil groups including the gifted and talented population. These strategies must be suitably challenging and varied, incorporating the breadth, depth and pace required to progress high achievement. Independent learning opportunities and the innovative use of ICT should be incorporated into all strategies to raise the achievement and motivation of gifted and talented pupils.

SCHOOL POLICY FRAMEWORK FOR GIFTED EDUCATION

Most schools already have a number of policies in place, and there will be a recognised format for these. Any policy for provision for gifted education should follow this format, and contain links and specific references to other school policies. A whole school policy for gifted educational provision should reflect both national and local initiatives and priorities, linking these to the ethos of the individual school and to the wider community. In the rationale or 'vision' statement that introduces a school policy, reference should be made to how the policy links into the school's general aims and philosophy and say why such a policy is necessary. The aims of making provision for gifted and talented pupils' access to appropriate education experiences should be clearly stated, perhaps including:

- identification of giftedness;
- creating opportunities to develop specific skills or talents;
- arrangements to allow pupils to work at higher levels than age peers;
- access to specialist teaching in particular areas.

The policy should contain definitions of giftedness and talent that reflect both national and local terminology, but set in the context of the school, setting out clear guidelines for the identification of giftedness and referring to specific materials to be used to support this process, including details of checklists or standardised tests to be used, and copies of questionnaires.

Organisational strategics and approaches should refer to whole school approaches to provision such as acceleration, curriculum compacting, specialist tuition and mentoring. Teaching and learning should refer to the strategies to be considered across the curriculum including issues linked to underachievement, for example: differentiation strategies in subject classes; homework policies; enrichment activities; learning styles and thinking skills; and ICT use. Extra-curricular provision should ideally list activities specially arranged to provide support and appropriately challenging activities for gifted and talented pupils, including enrichment programmes, residential experiences, after-school activities, performance arts tuition and productions, and competitions.

There should be a timeline for implementation of school policy, specifying staff responsibilities within the curricular framework of the school, and making suggestions for continuing professional development for staff so that they can implement teaching and learning strategies in their own subjects. Responsibility for co-ordinating and monitoring progress should be identified, perhaps naming a co-ordinator of gifted and talented provision, giving a clear outline of this role and listing responsibilities.

Monitoring and evaluation arrangements would look at the effectiveness of procedures for identification of gifted pupils, details of specific provision made for them and arrangements for monitoring achievement in subject departments or faculties.

PROVISION FOR GIFTED AND TALENTED PUPILS AT SECONDARY SCHOOL

Provision in any one school should be set within the context of school policies for 'teaching and learning' and 'gifted and talented'. If the core of gifted education is normal classroom teaching as part of a curriculum for excellence and improving attainment, every school should make provision that recognises individual differences and meets a variety of needs within this curriculum for the gifted as well as the least able pupils, and deploy a range of grouping approaches that reflect the varying needs of their pupils. Curriculum flexibility for educating gifted and talented pupils could include opportunities for them to progress more rapidly than their age group, perhaps taking external examinations early. Teachers may need to take a differentiated approach to delivering the subject curriculum, using a mixture of whole class, individual/small group and enrichment activities, with an increasing emphasis on individualised programmes for gifted pupils as they progress through the school and their interests become more specialised.

Those responsible for monitoring and evaluation of a school's provision for gifted and talented pupils might look for:

- procedures for identifying gifted and talented pupils, including awareness of underachievement and its causes;

- teaching and learning policy and approaches that provide for the needs of gifted and talented pupils, especially re teachers' expectations, teaching styles, and the selection of appropriately challenging resources activities and tasks;

- awareness of teachers of the additional needs of gifted and talented pupils and willingness to adapt their teaching to meet these;

- how the school matches its curriculum to the needs of gifted and talented pupils, and their access to specialist tuition, mentors, study support, out of school activities and master classes;

- whether pupils' achievements match their potential ability.

Gifted and talented pupils are more likely to reveal their abilities when schools take an inclusive approach, and teachers not only plan to meet the needs of those already identified as gifted and talented, but also contribute to the identification of others whose abilities are less obvious, perhaps being masked by disaffection, disadvantage or disability.

SUPPORT FOR GIFTED AND TALENTED PUPILS AT SECONDARY SCHOOL

A senior member of the teaching staff, with additional training in gifted education and close links to the senior management team, might be identified to be responsible for the co-ordination of provision for gifted and talented pupils. This co-ordinator's role could be based on the model for supporting pupils who have special educational needs, and in some schools the two roles are combined as provision for additional support for pupils. Whatever model is chosen by schools, this member of staff should link with subject heads of department and those responsible for school policies on teaching and learning, assessment, examinations, homework, extra-curricular provision and parental involvement to:

- assist subject staff with the identification of giftedness;
- manage the implementation of the school policy for gifted and talented pupils;
- provide practical help, advice and guidance to pupils, staff and parents;
- monitor gifted and talented pupils' achievement and attainment in co-operation with subject staff;
- arrange continuing professional development opportunities for colleagues, and participate in collegial discussion sessions;
- support subject teachers in planning lessons, and provide resources including ICT, to ensure appropriate differentiation in the curriculum;
- keep up with research and attend training in gifted education;
- encourage staff to provide resources and support for pupils' independent learning;
- ensure transfer of information at transition stages;
- foster links with outside agencies and co-ordinators in other schools;
- demonstrate good classroom practice in teaching gifted and talented pupils.

The senior management team may provide support for the school's gifted education provision by:

- ensuring staff awareness of key issues in the education of gifted and talented pupils;
- promoting staff training on gifted educational provision;
- identifying a member of staff to have co-ordinating responsibility for gifted and talented pupils;
- referring to provision for gifted and talented pupils in the school prospectus and subject department policies;
- ensuring that a whole-school policy for gifted pupils is in place along with the use of identification procedures to enable appropriate provision for them and that it is readily understood by all staff, pupils and parents;
- devising a range of strategies available across the curriculum to meet the emerging needs of gifted pupils and to celebrate the individuality of all pupils and appreciate their achievements.

SCHOOL–PARENT PARTNERSHIPS

These are essential to the support of gifted and talented pupils. Schools should:

- publish their policy for gifted education in the school's prospectus;
- have a system in place that enables parents to identify their children's abilities and achievements in out-of-school activities;

- provide advice and information about identification strategies used;

- describe curriculum provision that may be put in place for gifted and talented pupils;

- address any parental concerns about social development and behaviour;

- provide guidance and advice to parents about links to national associations and organisations for gifted and talented pupils;

- issue information about competitions, events or activities;

- include parents in extra-curricular activities such as visits to art galleries, theatres, museums and other places that may stimulate interest.

IMPLEMENTING POLICIES

Policies are usually determined by governments, local education authorities or individual schools. Some policies do not easily translate into classroom practice, while others may lead to confusion and inconsistency, especially if they are linked to funding and resource provision. For example, if local authorities or individual schools interpret rigidly government guidance to identify a percentage of pupils as gifted, this could create confusion and lead to anomalies, for example, when pupils move from low-achieving schools where they are classified as gifted to different areas where they do not fall within the top percentage, resulting in removal of their 'gifted' status.

It is important that all schools have systems in place to identify gifted and talented pupils in all subjects and year groups, with a shared understanding of agreed definitions in school, local and national contexts, that makes use of multiple criteria and sources of evidence to identify gifts and talents. If pupils meet these criteria, then they may be identified as gifted, and those who do not meet all of the criteria should be offered opportunities to develop their specific abilities.

Whether educational provision is determined by central government, local authorities or individual schools, there are common themes:

- identification of gifted pupils;

- provision for gifted pupils that supports the development of their abilities;

- teacher training to ensure that identification and provision are appropriately delivered at a school level.

Good practice should be innovative, but built on existing practice in the school with clearly stated objectives and a plan of action linked to raising attainment for all pupils.

Timeline of UK initiatives in gifted education

Note: While there are differences in terminology and in the organisation and structure of the curriculum across the countries in the United Kingdom, developments in the provision of gifted education follow a broadly similar pattern.

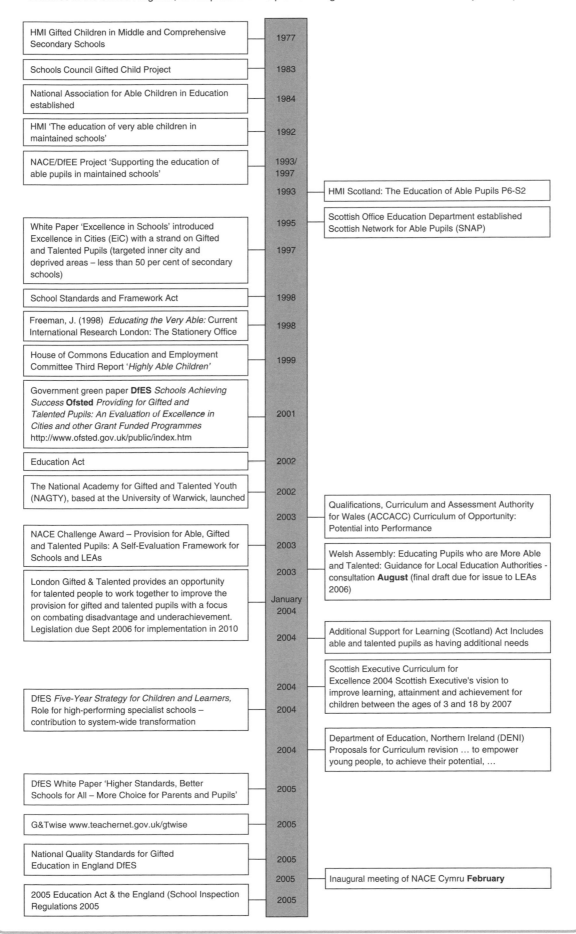

Year	England/UK	Year	Scotland/Wales/Northern Ireland
1977	HMI Gifted Children in Middle and Comprehensive Secondary Schools		
1983	Schools Council Gifted Child Project		
1984	National Association for Able Children in Education established		
1992	HMI 'The education of very able children in maintained schools'		
1993/1997	NACE/DfEE Project 'Supporting the education of able pupils in maintained schools'		
		1993	HMI Scotland: The Education of Able Pupils P6–S2
1995	White Paper 'Excellence in Schools' introduced Excellence in Cities (EiC) with a strand on Gifted and Talented Pupils (targeted inner city and deprived areas – less than 50 per cent of secondary schools)	1995	Scottish Office Education Department established Scottish Network for Able Pupils (SNAP)
1997			
1998	School Standards and Framework Act		
1998	Freeman, J. (1998) *Educating the Very Able:* Current International Research London: The Stationery Office		
1999	House of Commons Education and Employment Committee Third Report '*Highly Able Children*'		
2001	Government green paper **DfES** *Schools Achieving Success* **Ofsted** *Providing for Gifted and Talented Pupils: An Evaluation of Excellence in Cities and other Grant Funded Programmes* http://www.ofsted.gov.uk/public/index.htm		
2002	Education Act		
2002	The National Academy for Gifted and Talented Youth (NAGTY), based at the University of Warwick, launched		
		2003	Qualifications, Curriculum and Assessment Authority for Wales (ACCACC) Curriculum of Opportunity: Potential into Performance
2003	NACE Challenge Award – Provision for Able, Gifted and Talented Pupils: A Self-Evaluation Framework for Schools and LEAs	2003	Welsh Assembly: Educating Pupils who are More Able and Talented: Guidance for Local Education Authorities - consultation **August** (final draft due for issue to LEAs 2006)
January 2004	London Gifted & Talented provides an opportunity for talented people to work together to improve the provision for gifted and talented pupils with a focus on combating disadvantage and underachievement. Legislation due Sept 2006 for implementation in 2010	2004	Additional Support for Learning (Scotland) Act Includes able and talented pupils as having additional needs
2004	DfES *Five-Year Strategy for Children and Learners,* Role for high-performing specialist schools – contribution to system-wide transformation	2004	Scottish Executive Curriculum for Excellence 2004 Scottish Executive's vision to improve learning, attainment and achievement for children between the ages of 3 and 18 by 2007
		2004	Department of Education, Northern Ireland (DENI) Proposals for Curriculum revision … to empower young people, to achieve their potential, …
2005	DfES White Paper 'Higher Standards, Better Schools for All – More Choice for Parents and Pupils'		
2005	G&Twise www.teachernet.gov.uk/gtwise		
2005	National Quality Standards for Gifted Education in England DfES	2005	Inaugural meeting of NACE Cymru **February**
2005	2005 Education Act & the England (School Inspection Regulations 2005		

📖 FURTHER READING

Riley, T., Bevan-Brown, J., Bicknell, B., Carroll-Lind, J. and Kearney, A. (2004) *The Extent, Nature and Effectiveness of Planned Approaches in New Zealand Schools for Providing for Gifted and Talented Students.* Wellington NZ: New Zealand Ministry of Education, p. 11, electronic version retrieved on 12 May 2005 at http://www.minedu.govt.nz/

USEFUL WEBSITES

European Council for High Ability http://www.echa.ws/modules/
New South Wales Parents & Citizens' Federation Gifted Students Policy 2000 *Federation Annual Conference* http://www.austega.com/gifted/NSWPCPolicy. htm

Chapter 6

Teaching and Learning

This chapter looks at:

- Curriculum design
- Structured tinkering
- Curricular models
- Individualising the curriculum
- Learning styles
- Accelerated learning
- Learning to learn
- Thinking skills
- Thinking actively in a social context (TASC)

To provide appropriate support and challenge for gifted pupils in mixed ability classes, teachers should identify specific methodologies and consider the likely impact of these on both the content of the curriculum and its delivery (Renzulli and Reis, 1997).

CURRICULUM DESIGN

Principles for curriculum design require pupils to make progress in their learning over a range of contexts and the provision of challenge and opportunities that develop the capacity for different types of learning and thinking. The curriculum should be able to respond to individual needs and support particular aptitudes and talents (Scottish Executive, 2004). Teachers need to manage teaching and learning flexibly to find the right blend and balance for individual pupils, and schools may have to look beyond their own resources and expertise to make suitable provision for gifted and talented pupils.

STRUCTURED TINKERING

'... *systematic approach to the modification of the basic school curriculum to meet the needs of gifted and talented pupils.' (Eyre, 2002b)*

There is no single model of appropriate teaching for gifted pupils and many approaches to curriculum design are too rigid to meet the range of learning needs in mainstream secondary classrooms. Teachers should determine methodologies for curriculum change by looking at pupils' opportunities to demonstrate ability in their subject, evaluating this, then developing strategies that are tailored to meet the needs of each pupil identified as gifted. This should take into account three factors:

- Any improvement will include opportunities for enrichment, extension and acceleration 'threaded through' the curriculum.

- There is no single style of learning that meets the needs of gifted and talented pupils, since preferences are linked to personality rather than ability, so teaching approaches should be designed to respond to all learning styles.

- A school's learning context may be built on the skills and strategies of individual teachers, so effective approaches in one school may not work well in others.

Eyre's 'structured tinkering' approach (2002b) makes sense to teachers because it acknowledges their professional skills and takes account of the complexity of teaching and learning. It is an inclusive and relatively inexpensive approach to addressing issues of curriculum continuity and progression, while enabling gifted and talented pupils to feel less isolated within the school community. Individual teachers, by incorporating systematic modification and enhancement of areas of the curriculum, can adopt differentiation methodologies that meet the needs of gifted pupils while responding to the learning needs of the whole class. Instead of separating gifted pupils from their classmates, 'structured tinkering' empowers teachers to use existing skills and knowledge to embed provision for their gifted pupils within the classroom.

CURRICULAR MODELS

Many teaching strategies should be used by teachers to develop the gifts and talents of secondary pupils and tailored to the needs of pupils in their subject. Acceleration may be better than enrichment for some pupils, extraction for specialist tutoring may suit others, while effective challenge through differentiation meets the needs of a larger group.

Strategies for providing appropriate learning experiences for gifted pupils might include:

- *differentiation of the curriculum,* providing a range and variety of resources, tasks, support or groupings within subjects;

- *choice and variety* of subject activities involving several levels of challenge, enabling teachers to respond to the individual needs of pupils by modification of the curriculum;

- *a tailored curriculum* devised and adapted to meet the individual needs of gifted pupils as they arise;

- *acceleration*, where pupils are advanced in all areas by missing a year or more, or by covering one subject's content more rapidly;

- *curriculum telescoping or compacting*, where pupils progress through subject content faster and teachers offer only new material, instead of spending time on revision of topics already mastered (Reis and Renzulli, undated);

- *enrichment strategies*, encompassing additional input and 'extra' activities that may be either embedded in the curriculum, 'bolted on' as inserts, or provided out of school through clubs or visits to galleries, concerts and theatre;

- *short-term extraction* from class for tuition in a specific skill or subject within or additional to the context of the curriculum;

- *specialist provision*, including attendance at specialist schools and units where group work at an advanced level is essential, like sport and music;

- *independent/individualised study*, including e-learning to access specialist help or mentors, with pupils undertaking specially designed courses that meet clearly identified needs.

School ethos, policies and timetabling approaches may impact on the nature of the provision for gifted and talented pupils. Some provision for gifted education is inclusive and incorporated into the design of the curriculum, and some is 'bolted-on', perhaps failing to link with subject-based classroom learning, which can result in a lack of continuity and progression. Providers of 'extra' programmes may lack knowledge of the classroom context, leading to repetition of work or to some gifted pupils finding the mainstream curriculum boring as a result of different experiences in an enrichment activity. Extraction from the subject class in order to participate in enrichment programmes may result in gifted pupils becoming isolated from their classmates or losing touch with the core curriculum.

INDIVIDUALISING THE CURRICULUM

The content of the secondary curriculum consists largely of various subject facts, concepts, problems and themes, and gifted pupils cover this material at a rapid pace, dealing well with abstractions. They often have different interests from their classmates, so need to work at different levels, at a faster pace and with different materials, creating a need for teachers to devise individualised educational programmes that may include:

- content involving more and deeper knowledge, with less time spent on revision of material already covered;

- metacognition and study/thinking skills programmes to support independent study;

- specialised e-learning or out of school programmes.

Individualised educational programmes should identify pupils' strengths and development needs and outline arrangements to meet these, enabling teachers and pupils to set appropriately challenging learning targets, with clear goals and structure.

LEARNING STYLES

Traditionally, school subjects have been taught using an approach that relies on learning by listening and writing, so pupils whose natural learning style is not suited to this approach may not learn effectively. There are many instruments available to help determine pupils' preferred learning styles, using questionnaires or charts like preferred learning styles on p. 53, derived from the work of Rose (1985), but it is possible for teachers and pupils to identify these by simple observation:

- *Visual learners* often look at the teacher's face intently, make lists to help organise their thoughts and recall information by remembering how it was set out on a page.

- *Auditory-verbal* learners prefer verbal instructions, solve problems by talking about them, use sound as a memory aid and enjoy discussions.

- *Kinaesthetic learners* learn best when they are active, finding it difficult to sit still for long periods, and they may use movement as a memory aid.

- *Tactile learners* learn well in hands-on activities like projects and demonstrations and prefer to use writing and drawing as memory aids.

Pupils seem to learn better and more quickly if the teaching methods used match their preferred learning styles, so teachers need to be aware not only of the learning styles of their pupils, but also of their own teaching style, in order to be able to adapt their methods and activities. If teachers vary the activities they use in lessons, and ensure that there is a reasonable balance of these to suit all four modalities of learners, they will cater for all pupils some of the time.

Visual learners will be able to recall what they see and will prefer written instructions. These pupils can visualise information as pictures, enjoy reading silently and prefer to study in a quiet place away from visual disturbances. Their strengths include:

- use of colour highlighters to organise notes and identify key information;

- brainstorming, using illustrations, mind maps and models;

- skim-reading to get an overview before reading in detail.

Auditory learners will be able to recall what they hear and will prefer oral instructions. They learn by listening and speaking and enjoy talking and interviewing. They are phonetic readers who enjoy oral reading, choral reading, and listening to recorded books. Their strengths include:

- use of voice recorder instead of, or as well as, making notes;

- creation of musical jingles and mnemonics to aid memory;

- explaining aloud while they write their ideas down.

Tactile and kinaesthetic learners learn best by touching or manipulating objects, and take frequent study breaks. They understand instructions that they write and learn best using flow charts and mind mapping. They enjoy hands-on manipulation, carrying out experiments and doing practical tasks. Their strengths include:

- using colours to highlight reading material, making posters or models;

- being able to multi-task, moving around to learn new things.

If gifted and talented pupils do not appear to fit clearly into one of the four common modes, Gardner's (1993) theories of multiple intelligences and Honey and Mumford's (1986) self-test may provide a more detailed picture of individual pupils' learning preferences.

There are some general characteristics of gifted pupils that may contribute to their preferred learning styles:

- Some gifted pupils are spontaneous and intuitive and do not like to be bored. They prefer curriculum content to be presented in an interesting manner with attractive materials, and learn best through co-operative learning strategies.

- Others are logical and prefer to plan and organise their work. They learn best when lessons are structured and information is presented in sequential steps so they can work independently.

No matter how teachers identify pupils' preferred learning styles, when the way they teach closely matches the way pupils like to learn, results can improve significantly and the likelihood of underachievement is reduced (McKay, 2004).

ACCELERATED LEARNING

Accelerated learning programmes are designed to help pupils improve memory by using techniques that actively involve the brain, and require teachers to motivate their pupils using multiple intelligences and preferred learning styles. Developed from the theory of multiple intelligences (Gardner, 1993) and research into the brain (Smith, 1998), this strategy involves teachers knowing about how people learn in order to design more effective classroom learning experiences. An accelerated learning programme begins with teachers creating supportive learning environments that include interventions to remove pupils' anxiety and stress as well as measures to maintain positive self-esteem. Essential lesson content includes:

- connecting a new topic to what pupils already know and introducing the learning outcomes;

- explicitly explaining lesson content and processes to encourage metacognition;

- using the preferred learning styles of the pupils utilising a multiple intelligences approach;

- reviewing for recall and retention.

Accelerated learning may be characterised by the use of music in the classroom; Mozart's music is thought to co-ordinate breathing, cardiovascular rhythm and brain wave rhythm.

LEARNING TO LEARN

Any teaching strategy designed to improve pupils' learning in an inclusive setting will impact on gifted pupils who are already good learners, and they might become even better learners if they understand how they learn. Cognitive apprenticeship (Clark and Callow, 2002) encourages and motivates learning through:

- ensuring that pupils understand the purpose of their learning;
- providing opportunities for pupils to talk about learning;
- promoting goal setting by the pupils;
- encouraging co-operation and competition between pupils.

Expert pupil performance might be developed by:

- *Coaching*: providing feedback and identifying role models to help pupils towards expert performance.
- *Scaffolding*: a system of stimulation and support by the teacher gradually reduced as pupils become more expert.
- *Articulation*: pupils are given the chance to explain their reasoning.
- *Reflection*: pupils are given the chance to compare their thinking processes with others.
- *Exploration*: pupils come up with their own problem solutions.

As with accelerated learning, the use of multiple intelligences and preferred learning styles, this strategy is designed to develop and improve the way pupils acquire and demonstrate knowledge.

THINKING SKILLS

Thinking skills are part of all good teaching and learning and help pupils to develop initiative and enterprise in how they learn and meet challenges effectively.

In the secondary school, pupils learn subject content, and there is less emphasis on teaching the process of learning. Details of any thinking skills programmes used in local primaries may not be known, so continuity of approach is lost, along with pupils' ability to employ the skills acquired. Some subject teachers introduce thinking skills inserts, and, though these are often highly successful, they may not become embedded in teaching and learning generally and the skills taught may not transfer to other contexts. Sometimes thinking skills techniques used in primary school are rejected by pupils as 'babyish' and unsuitable for secondary subject work; there is a clear need for primary and secondary schools to work together to identify a shared framework for developing thinking skills in the curriculum. Adopting a whole-school framework would reduce confusion and have an increased chance of success, since pupils would experience the same methodology in every classroom, making the transfer of skills from one context to another more likely. Primary school colleagues could be involved, either by passing information about their metacognition or thinking skills programmes to secondary colleagues, or by collaborative working where teachers from both sectors develop or adopt a programme.

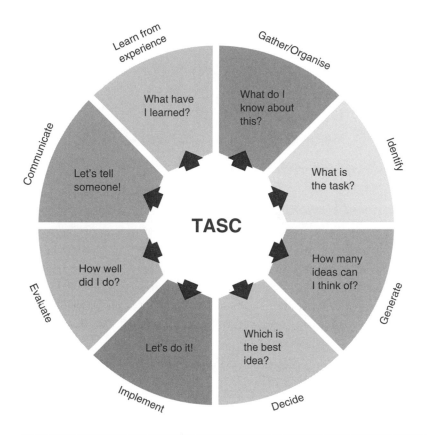

Figure 6.1 TASC: Thinking Actively in a Social Context The TASC Problem-solving Wheel Wallace (2004)

THINKING ACTIVELY IN A SOCIAL CONTEXT (TASC)

Wallace and Adams (1993) developed a generic framework for the development of a thinking and problem-solving curriculum in an inclusive setting which recognises that pupils learn best in a social environment in which they can give meaning to their own experiences. This framework advocates a whole-school approach to the development of thinking and problem-solving across a range of abilities that, used consistently across the curriculum, would lead to skills being more easily transferred across subjects. The TASC problem-solving wheel was devised to illustrate this approach (see Figure 6.1).

Using the TASC wheel incorporates three distinct stages:

1 *Identify the problem*: the pupils clarify the task and establish its purpose, using their own words.

2 *Produce ideas*: all members of the group suggest possible solutions to the problem and discuss how to proceed.

3 *Find solutions to the problem*: pupils select and implement their solutions and determine what worked best.

It is used to break stages into smaller steps:

- *Gather and organise*: establish what is already known.
- *Identify*: define the problem.
- *Generate* alternative solutions to the problem.
- *Decide* which of the initial ideas is best and consider possible consequences.
- *Implement* the chosen idea, using a variety of methods.
- *Evaluate* how well the idea worked and look at alternatives, try out then evaluate these.
- *Communicate*: establish an audience and report on the activity.
- *Learn from experience*: reflect on the problem-solving process.

The teaching of thinking skills or metacognition involves letting pupils do most of the work, and they often cannot do it at first. They need support, but they also need teachers to resist the temptation to make it easier, ending up with the teacher 'doing the thinking' and working very hard while the pupils sit back and wait to be provided with the answers. This process can work successfully with a group of underachieving, disaffected pupils.

Whether particular strategies are adopted by the whole school, a department or an individual teacher, the needs of gifted and talented pupils may be met in the classroom by the provision of a challenging learning environment that takes account of the range of pupils' learning styles and involves the informed use of diverse and flexible teaching styles and resources (Teare, 1997).

This chart may help you find your learning style; read the left column and then choose the best answer from the other columns. The column where most of your answers appear gives your preferred learning style. (Based on Colin Rose (1987) *Accelerated Learning*.)

	Visual	Auditory	Kinaesthetic & Tactile
Reading	Do you like descriptive scenes and imagine the actions?	Do you enjoy dialogue and hear the characters talk?	Do you not like fiction and prefer true stories?
Spelling	Do you try to see the word?	Do you sound out the word or use a phonetic approach?	Do you write the word down to find if it feels right?
Talking	Do you use words like see and imagine? Do you not talk much or like listening for long?	Do you use words such as hear and think? Do you enjoy listening but like to talk or interrupt?	Do you use words such as feel and touch? Do you use gestures and make faces?
Concentrating	Are you distracted by mess or movement?	Are you distracted by sounds or noise?	Are you distracted by activity going on around you?
Meeting someone you know	Do you forget names but remember faces or where you met?	Do you forget faces but remember names or what you talked about?	Do you remember best what you did together?
Trying something new	Do you like to see demonstrations, diagrams or posters?	Do you prefer verbal instructions or talking about it with someone?	Do you prefer to get right down to try it?
Making or building something	Do you look at the instructions and the picture?	Do you ask someone for advice?	Do you ignore the instructions and work it out as you go?
Needing help	Do you look for help pages or diagrams?	Do you ask someone for help, or talk yourself through it?	Do you keep trying to figure it out by trial and error?

 Photocopiable: Supporting Gifted and Talented Pupils in the Secondary School
Paul Chapman Publishing 2006 © Moira Thomson

Thinking actively in a social context (TASC)

Background

TASC was introduced to a group of 14-year-old pupils identified as underachieving in formal classroom settings, who sometimes experienced difficulties with relationships, behaviour and attitude.

Introducing TASC

At the beginning of each lesson, pupils participated in a 'check-in' when they could comment positively or negatively about their emotional response to events of the previous week. The teacher placed importance on building up the concept of a whole-class team, even though pupils worked in small groups that were changed at times to ensure that everyone had the opportunity to participate and develop individuals' ability to work with different partners.

Pupils were encouraged to identify their preferred learning styles, using a questionnaire, but this failed to determine useful results as most ticked almost every box. Then they were given a set of secondary curriculum subject cards and asked to put them in order of preference from 'most comfortable', then to find classmates who had chosen the same type of subjects. Pupils engaged more effectively with this approach, and it was then used as the basis for some group tasks.

The TASC wheel was introduced after six weeks, generating discussion of this approach, and pupils were excited though uncertain of taking on responsibility for their own learning.

Brainstorming was introduced as a way of gathering and organising ideas, and pupils devised rules to ensure a 'professional' attitude:

- Everyone must take part.
- Everyone must be encouraged to take part.
- All ideas are written down – even the daft ones!
- No one is made to feel bad about any ideas they give.
- One person needs to record the ideas of others in the group – but they must also put forward ideas.

Carousel activity

A question was placed at the top of a sheet of paper on four separate tables. Pupils travelled in groups around the four questions, writing down answers to the question, each group using a different colour. If they agreed with other groups' answers they could indicate this by ticking the response; if they disagreed they could put an X beside the response; if they needed more information they put a question mark.

Teacher reflection

Pupils engaged really well with the carousel – the movement and speed of the task had a positive effect. Active participation was very high, as all pupils contributed to most questions. Ideas that were intended to provoke were vetoed by other groups who placed crosses against them – it is unlikely that pupils would have been able to express negatives in an open discussion situation, for fear of being rebuffed by peers. Almost all answers were approved, while answers suggesting a lack of understanding of the question were identified. This appeared to clarify pupils' thinking. Pupils agreed that the carousel had been an effective way of making sure everyone's ideas were heard.

At pupils' request, team-building activities designed to build up concentration skills were introduced. Pupils were asked to:

- organise themselves in order of height;
- remember the pupil on their left and right;
- organise themselves into a circle at random;
- pass a ball around the circle from tallest to shortest;
- introduce a second ball to follow the first;
- introduce a third ball, passed in the opposite direction.

The group worked as a team for the organisation task and successfully completed stages one and two of the game, demonstrating their sense of achievement by spontaneous applause, but did not successfully complete the third stage.

The groups were then encouraged to select an activity where they felt they could do well:

- Design a poster to demonstrate brainstorming guidelines.
- Design a questionnaire for pupils and staff to complete.
- Participate in a planning group.

(See help sheets reproduced on pages 57–8.)

The questionnaire and planning groups worked efficiently as teams, with high levels of motivation and good approaches to problem solving, but the brainstorming group had no clear idea of what they were doing so they used the help sheet to plan what they needed to do. All pupils showed improved motivation and concentration on the task, enabling them to work independently.

Pupils then took time for further team building and to reflect and plan ahead:

- The TASC wheel was reintroduced.
- They were encouraged to reflect on their progress.
- Consideration was given to the next steps by prioritising and revising tasks in hand.

Having agreed to tackle the issue of litter in the school environment, or 'The Street', several ideas were considered. Pupils eventually agreed to:

1 Make a video of:

- interviews of pupils from group;
- interviews of dinner ladies, a school cleaner and the janitor/caretaker;
- footage of 'The Street' before and after morning interval.

2   Arrange a 'Smarten up our school' week.

3   Compose a rubbish rap:

- group interested in doing this to be identified;
- words and music to be put together;
- finished rap to be included in the video.
- no – would reveal identity.

All of these activities were implemented, resulting in a high-profile anti-litter campaign supported by video material and the performance of the rubbish rap.

Pupils planning grid

Our Ideas	What we need to carry it out	Time it will take	How will we know it's working
Do a survey to find out what other people think	Questionnaire	One period to make up	Questionnaire completed on time
	Permission – time/place to get questionnaire completed	One week to get it completed	At least 2 classes per year group have completed it
	A place to show results	One period to evaluate and present results	?????????
Introduce Novelty Bins	Research companies for availability & costing	One period	Companies identified and approached
	Permission from Head Teacher	One period to gather & present information to HT	Permission agreed
	Funding to purchase bins	One period to approach possible funding sources Lunch time to work on Newsletter as source for funding	Funding sources identified Appropriate sources approached Newsletter published and sold
Gather Evidence to support our compaign	Photograph litter around the school	One period to take photographs	Photographs taken
	Display photographs in the street	One period to put together display	Photographs pupils looking at photos Ask pupils what they think of them

CONTINUED

Pupils then composed and delivered a presentation of their experiences to an invited audience at their local university.

Teacher's reflection

- Level of co-operation among pupils much higher.
- Level of independent activity, i.e. without direct teacher support, much higher.
- Standard of work improved, noticeable in the quality of responses.
- Pupils now taking responsibility for 'feeding back' on activities.
- More forward planning going on, with pupils identifying next steps.

Achieving success

The group received lots of positive feedback, which meant that the level of perceived success was very high. The school development planning group took up the issue of improving the school environment as a direct result of raised awareness, and an 'eco group' was proposed to take the group's initiatives further. The pupils were asked to design fliers reminding pupils to clear up. The group was nominated for the *'Standing Up to Antisocial Behaviour Awards Scheme'* – any award to go towards the purchase of novelty bins for 'The Street'.

Help sheets

Brainstorming

Use this sheet to help you think about your ideas and choose the best ones.
Reminder Your poster must include:

- Words
- Pictures
- Drawings
- Colours
- Catch-phrase or slogan

Tick items you have included in your poster.

Brainstorming Guidelines

Write your ideas down under each guideline – this way you can be sure you have met the criteria for the task, and have thought through your ideas to make sure you have chosen the best one.

1. Everyone must take part.
2. Everyone must be encouraged to take part.
3. All ideas are written down – even the daft ones!!!
4. No one is made to feel bad about any ideas they give.
5. One person needs to record the ideas of others in the group.
6. An awareness of why brainstorming is a good way to begin a task.

***

Planning

The planning stage is crucial to any campaign. It's very tempting just to jump in and get started, particularly if you think you have a really good idea.

Here are some suggestions for your group to think about:

CONTINUED

- You need to research novelty bin availability – who supplies them?
- You need to research costs involved – how many bins would we need?
- You need to convince your head teacher that it's a good idea – how will you do this?
- You need to identify staff willing to support your idea – have you thought about asking for funding from Enterprise?
- Perhaps gathering evidence to support your plan might be helpful – how could you do this?
- It is a good idea to allocate tasks to group members – this spreads the load and makes sure everything gets done.

* * *

Questionnaire Design

You have a very difficult task, and one which you need to give a bit of thought to.

Here are some suggestions which your group might want to consider:

- Do some research on the Internet to find examples of questionnaires.
- It doesn't really matter what these questionnaires are about, they will help you decide on the look (format) of your questionnaire.
- However, you might find some about litter which you could adapt for your own purposes – print these off and pick out the best ones.
- Use the 'brainstorming' technique to get as many questions as you can – remember, all ideas should be jotted down.
- Revise the results of the brainstorming and choose the best questions.
- It is very important to think ahead – try to imagine the completed questionnaire and think about the work involved in organising the results and using them to support your campaign to reduce litter in The Street.

📖 FURTHER READING

De Bono, E. (1992) *Six Thinking Hats for Schools*. Cheltenham, Australia: Hawker Brownlow

Fisher, R. (2002) *Thinking Skills: Adding Challenge to the Curriculum*. A guide for teachers of able children. Glasgow: Scottish Network for Able Pupils

Honey, P. and Mumford, A. (1986) *The Manual of Learning Styles*. London: BBC Books

McGuinness, C. (1999) *From Thinking Skills to Thinking Classrooms: A Review and Evaluation of Approaches for Developing Pupils' Thinking*. Nottingham: DfEE Publications.

Williams, S. (2004) 'Taking the Right Steps', *Teaching Thinking and Creativity* (14): 5–11

Wilson, V. (2000) *Can Thinking Skills Be Taught?* Appendix 3, Scottish Executive Education Department Forum on Thinking Skills held in Edinburgh, May 2000, electronic version accessed 4 May 2005 at http://www.scre.ac.uk/scot-research/thinking/index.html

USEFUL WEBSITE

http://www.ablepupils.org
http://www.dfes.gov.uk/research/data/uploadfiles/RB115.doc
http://www.scre.ac.uk/scot-research/thinking/index.html

Part II

Specific Strategies

Chapter 7

Differentiation

This chapter looks at:

- Qualitative differentiation for gifted and talented pupils
- Strategies for subject curriculum differentiation
- Differentiation by homework
- Differentiation by e-learning
- Differentiation by challenge
- A language homework programme
- Web portals for e-learning
- Heriot-Watt University, Edinburgh: SCHOLAR Programme
- The Pushkin Prizes

Curriculum differentiation for gifted pupils involves making changes in the depth, breadth and pace of pupils' learning (McClure, 2001) that may be enhanced with the use of appropriate classroom management strategies, varied teaching styles, flexible grouping and support, and the availability of a wide range of resources. Curriculum organisation should be flexible, with provision for enrichment and subject choice, while offering opportunities to pupils that will enable them to work beyond their age and/or stage according to their aptitudes and interests.

QUALITATIVE DIFFERENTIATION FOR GIFTED AND TALENTED PUPILS

Qualitative differentiation (Renzulli, 1997a; Riley, 2004) is a term used by educators to describe teaching and learning experiences that are tailored to the needs of gifted and talented pupils. The strengths, interests and learning styles of these pupils underpin the introduction of strategies for individualising the curriculum and creating opportunities to design and implement programmes that meet their needs. For pupils to move through a subject curriculum at their own pace using more challenging material, teachers must determine what they already know, identify what they still need to learn, then replace the usual curriculum with new streamlined lessons, and provide acceleration and enrichment options.

Qualitative differentiation for gifted pupils will embody enrichment and acceleration together with curriculum compacting and flexible pacing. Enrichment generally refers to learning activities permitting broadening and deepening of the subject curriculum according to the abilities and needs of individual pupils, while acceleration refers to a more rapid pace of delivery and progress or the early introduction of content and skills. Both have potential advantages and disadvantages, and it is widely recognised that both should be used as complementary approaches to a qualitatively differentiated education.

STRATEGIES FOR SUBJECT CURRICULUM DIFFERENTIATION

Differentiation should not be viewed in simplistic terms as extra worksheets or one-off lessons. *Quantitative* differentiation (more of the same) should not be teachers' response to gifted pupils learning faster than their classmates. Renzulli, (1988). Established ways of differentiating the secondary subject curriculum that ensure its relevance and complexity to all pupils include:

- Use of tiered assignments (core and extension activities) that are designed to meet the needs of a group of learners functioning at a range of levels in the same class. Although all pupils work on broadly similar content, they may be asked different questions or provided with different tasks according to their known subject ability. Teachers employing this strategy must ensure that they provide appropriately challenging activities for gifted pupils, and not just the use of more complex materials.

- Creation of a flexible learning environment that encourages pupils to engage with the subject curriculum, build knowledge and skills and take risks.

- Introduction of workstations allowing pupils to move around, engage in activities designed to extend their understanding, introduce new processes and develop originality and creativity. Pupils complete all activities rapidly or work intensely on a single task, enabling the teacher to take account of pupils' different learning styles.

- Collaborative group work where pupils interact with one another and contribute a variety of expertise rather than all working on the same aspect of a project. Gifted pupils need opportunities for both individual and collaborative work, but they may be isolated within groups because of their ability level. Wallace and Bentley's (2002) TASC can facilitate a truly collaborative approach to inquiry-based open-ended tasks.

Most secondary teachers are accustomed to considering differentiation of the subject curriculum in terms of modification of content, process, product and the learning environment in order to enable gifted pupils to realise their potential. Several useful matrices in Gross et al. (2001) are based on research into differentiation and provide subject-specific examples of how the secondary curriculum can be modified to ensure appropriate challenge for gifted pupils, and Renzulli's (1988: et al., 2000) multiple menu model suggests several routes towards achieving a differentiated curriculum for the gifted. No matter which strategy is selected, subject teachers must endeavour to create a learning environment that provides appropriate challenge and support for all pupils, including those identified as gifted and talented.

Differentiation options include co-operative programmes designed to help teachers address the needs of advanced high-school pupils who undertake college-level coursework while still attending school. The International Baccalaureate (IB) is an international qualification taught in more than 100 countries around the world, involving intellectual rigour and high academic standards, with a strong emphasis on the ideals of international understanding and responsible citizenship. The IB Diploma Programme is available for pupils aged 16–18 who intend to go on to university and is a broad-based qualification that demonstrates the all-round academic ability of its graduates with the advantage of being an international qualification recognised in many countries.

DIFFERENTIATION BY HOMEWORK

One aim of differentiation for gifted pupils is to remove the ceiling on what is learned, and use pupils' abilities to build a more diverse and efficiently organised knowledge base. While it is virtually impossible for a single teacher to provide fully effective differentiation of content for gifted pupils within the mixed ability classroom, this can be supported by the development of homework programmes for gifted pupils. These might be devised by teachers for one or two gifted pupils, or developed by a subject department; materials might be used from more advanced levels of study, from commercially produced packages (for example, Teare, 1999, 2001) or specially written. Many teacher-designed homework tasks are produced in response to specific needs of individual pupils, but may grow into articulated programmes to meet needs that appear often in a subject area. Examples from one such programme, developed in response to an identified lack of grammatical rigour and pupils' lack of knowledge of etymology, are given on pages 65–7.

DIFFERENTIATION BY E-LEARNING

Appropriate information and communications technology (ICT) use facilitates the progress of gifted and talented pupils, allowing them to move through lower-order thinking rapidly and access higher-order thinking tasks involving cognitive challenge, critical thinking and problem solving. It is possible for individual pupils to participate in collaborative group work with others who are similarly gifted, providing them with an appropriate peer group electronically. Brainstorming and other techniques that encourage the use of intuitive, imaginative approaches and risk-taking are also possible using ICT, since software is non-judgemental, providing a safe environment that allows pupils to fail. Many ICT activities add acceleration and enrichment to differentiation of the subject curriculum, and the range of available resources is vast and easily enables effective curriculum differentiation for gifted pupils.

One very effective way of individualising the curriculum for all pupils, from the least able to the highly gifted, is to use interactive software that takes into account differing abilities and levels of prior knowledge, then provides pupils with personalised courses, continuously updated according to performance. This allows not only effective differentiation of subject process, but also of pace and material appropriate to pupils' needs, thus optimising their achievements. SuccessMaker Enterprise (see Useful websites at end of chapter) is one example of an integrated learning system designed to improve numeracy and literacy for pupils at all ability levels by:

- continually maintaining and developing skills – pupils work on a variety of activities, ensuring that learning is progressive;

- improving motivation and behaviour – pupils are encouraged and their successes rewarded, so raising self-esteem;

- supporting effective target-setting – detailed reports enable teachers to set appropriate targets for pupils and monitor progress.

Many schools use interactive software to help individualise the curriculum and raise educational standards; several case studies are available on the RM website.

There are many websites that can be used not only to differentiate but also to enrich pupils' learning, and a growing number of web portals provide links to specific websites. These are of particular value to busy teachers who need to check new websites to ensure that the material is relevant and appropriate and that the school's gatekeeper will permit pupils to access the site. Some portals cater specifically for gifted pupils, and details are given on pages 67–9.

E-mentoring is often a combination of the enrichment, acceleration and specialist tuition required for subject differentiation for gifted and talented pupils who need provision beyond the available resources and expertise of their subject teachers. The Heriot-Watt University SCHOLAR programme offers distance learning and computer-supported open learning to school pupils while providing educational resources and a 'virtual college' support network, with e-mentoring from under- and post-graduate students as well as teachers and university staff. Access to the programme is via the school, and flexible, imaginative use of this provision is encouraged by the University; many senior pupils use the interactive programmes to support their study for advanced examinations or even to earn credits towards exemptions on university courses, while use by younger pupils who are gifted in the subjects offered is encouraged. Some schools have enrolled junior pupils on the programme to allow them access to tuition and support at a level well beyond what is available in school, while others use distance learning to fill gaps in the school curriculum.

DIFFERENTIATION BY CHALLENGE

Competition is common in the classroom and many teachers deliberately encourage this in order to extract quality responses from their pupils. Whether challenge is offered through classroom quizzes and games or structured prize-bearing contests, competition provides a clear route to differentiation of product by:

- encouraging time-management skills and realistic planning;

- involving original manipulation of information rather than regurgitation of learned facts;

- self-evaluation using criteria that is defined within the rules of the contest;

- allowing gifted and motivated pupils to stimulate each other by being competitive and by co-operating towards the final product.

While many competitions like the BBC's Young Musician of the Year look for skilled specialist entrants and others provide enriching experiences for all pupils, competition to differentiate aspects of the secondary subject curriculum for gifted pupils may take the form of sports contests, performing arts auditions, 'Ready, Steady, Cook' challenges, entries for art exhibitions and many more, covering every aspect of the curriculum. Local, national and international competitions and challenges can provide enrichment for all pupils while at the same time offering curriculum differentiation for the gifted.

Personal and imaginative writing is an important element of the secondary school English curriculum and is almost always differentiated according to pupils' responses, but gifted young writers often require more challenge in order to stimulate their creativity and stretch their writing skills. It is a simple task to extend this to the production of writing that meets the challenge of a competition, and the Pushkin Prizes is an example of one prestigious competition available to 12/13-year-old writers in Scotland and Russia.

Teachers need to plan differentiated approaches for their gifted and talented pupils that exclude repetitive practice exercises which do not extend skills or ideas. The most sophisticated form of differentiation is in the relationships that teachers build with individual pupils and in the everyday interactions that occur in the classroom:

- demonstrating enthusiasm and knowledge about a subject;

- teaching strategies that support the various learning styles of individual gifted and talented pupils;

- open-questioning that develops pupils' thinking skills;

- supporting gifted and talented pupils to take risks in their learning.

Differentiated teaching and learning that is challenging and varied in breadth, depth and pace, offering both individual and group activities, can be used by all secondary subject teachers to support the development of independent learning skills in their pupils, and enable those identified as gifted and talented to progress to high achievement.

CASE STUDY

Differentiation by homework, secondary English

This homework programme supports differentiation of the secondary English curriculum and consists of activities designed for pupils who have already achieved beyond the required standard in the early years of secondary school. The activities are supported by fact sheets and require the use of numerous reference

CONTINUED

sources. Pupils may opt in to the programme at any stage in the first two years of secondary school.

Aims

- To develop pupils' awareness of the structure of the English language, including parts of speech and grammar.
- To extend pupils' knowledge of how the English language developed using roots, prefixes and suffixes.
- To enable pupils' exploration of the origin of various commonly used terms in order to gain a deeper understanding of how these came to be incorporated into the language and add to their understanding of literature.
- To make appropriate use of reference texts, computer software and on-line search engines.
- To apply a range of language skills in practical exercises.

Partnership with parents

Since this programme is additional to the normal homework of the school, parental support is important. Parents are given details of the aims and content of the programme and are asked to monitor pupils' homework to ensure that they are not being overloaded, as may happen when teachers try to challenge and support those considered to be gifted in their subject. It is not expected that pupils will necessarily complete homework activities in a single sitting – some might be appropriately spread over a week or more.

Content

Activities in the programme (see examples on pp. 74–6) are designed to support:

1   Reading for information:

- obtaining specific information from a text;
- gathering information for cross-curricular research;
- categorising appropriate information sources for particular purposes;
- making statements of the main ideas and purposes of text with reference to relevant content;
- relating detail of text to the overall context.

2   Punctuation and structure:

- accurate and varied paragraph and sentence construction;
- the manipulation of punctuation, paragraphing and sentence structures to achieve particular effects;
- the development of a sense of the importance of proof-reading.

3   Functional writing:

- collating information from a range of sources;
- ordering and presenting ideas and opinions with an attempt at reasoning;
- applying conventions of particular literary forms to achieve particular effects;
- selecting appropriate writing structures and formats to convey information;
- using a variety of forms of functional writing, including discursive and persuasive writing.

CONTINUED

4 Personal and imaginative writing:

- the exploration of more complex and original forms of writing through exposure to a variety of stylistic techniques and linguistic effects in personal reading;
- the use of the conventions of a chosen literary form;
- the use of language to achieve particular effects;
- demonstration of insight and self-awareness in personal writing;
- development of the changes in ideas, structure and vocabulary appropriate to different forms of personal writing;
- development of ways of selecting what is appropriate form, expressing reactions to and feelings about personal experiences in writing.

Resources and ICT

Adult support and access to a range of reference materials and ICT is offered at the after-school homework club to ensure that pupils undertaking the programme have full access to all resources that might contribute to their success and resulting attainment.

DIFFERENTIATION BY E-LEARNING: SOME EASY TO ACCESS PORTALS

1 **BECTA** – British Educational Communications and Technology Agency – is the leading UK agency for the delivery of ICT and e-strategies for schools at http://www.becta.org.uk/

BECTA provides links to school websites alongside governmental websites, such as the United States Environmental Protection Agency's information on acid rain.

BECTA publications are available to order on-line free to *UK residents*.

2 **National Grid for Learning** (http//www.ngfl.gov.uk/) is a gateway to quality assured educational resources on the Internet, providing a network of selected links to websites that offer high-quality content and information. The NGfL portal was launched in November 1998, as part of the UK Government's National Grid for Learning strategy to help learners and educators in the United Kingdom benefit from ICT. There are over 100 links to websites that range across the secondary school curriculum, and various games and quizzes may be found at http://www.ngfl.gov.uk/what. jsp?sec=2&cat=265&clear=y

3 **Curriculum Online** (http://www.curriculumonline.gov.uk/default.htm?cookie% 5Ftest=1) provides multimedia resources to support teaching and learning across the English school curriculum, allowing teachers to search for on-line materials in all curricular subjects, specifying year group and level of study as well as the specific aspect of the subject curriculum, for example:

Teaching subject: English – Shakespeare quizzes

Description: six on-line quizzes covering *Macbeth, Romeo and Juliet, Twelfth Night, Henry V, Shakespeare* and *Famous Quotes.* Test your knowledge and get instant feedback

Publisher: Carel Press (Publication date 1 January 2002)
Product type: Assessment
http://www.carelpress.co.uk/quizpage.htm
   This product is free from Carel Press.

4   **Hoagies' Gifted Education Page** (http://www.hoagiesgifted.org/) offers resources and links for parents, for educators, administrators and other professionals, and for children and teenagers.

5   **BBC Learning** (http://www.bbc.co.uk/learning) website provides links to resources for learners of all ages and at all levels, across the BBC's television and radio channels with a range of on-line courses.

6   **BBC Schools** (http://www.bbc.co.uk/schools/) provides interactive learning resources for children at home and at school, from early years to all ages and stages of the curriculum, including Bitesize. http://www.bbc.co.uk/schools/revision provides revision guides for the various examination levels for schools in England, Scotland and Wales.

7   **Onion Street** (http://www.bbc.co.uk/schools/communities/onionstreet/) is a school work support site for 11–16-year-olds. They can:

   ● get help with their work;

   ● quiz education experts;

   ● chat to people their own age;

   ● read and watch interviews with experts;

   ● get advice on revision technique and dealing with school stress;

   ● take a break in the music and art rooms.

8   **Exscitec** (http://www.exscitec.com/) develops and delivers high-calibre, hands-on problem-solving learning experiences, and delivers programmes to raise aspirations in the study of science, technology, engineering and maths (STEM) for pupils at various stages of the curriculum. As an extension of the partnership with Imperial College London, Exscitec works in collaboration with local education authorities and institutions in England to develop customised activities. Across its portfolio of programmes, Exscitec adapts learning objectives in order to cater for student groups with differing aptitudes.

9   **EnrichUK** (http://www.enrichuk.net/) is the gateway to a collection of 150 sites supported in the United Kingdom by the New Opportunities Fund. The collection ranges across culture, history, social and economic development, science and art as well as offering regional and national 'sense of place' websites from England, Scotland, Northern Ireland and Wales, the EnrichUK search engine delivering results for all active sites supported. People from all over the world may see over 30,000 objects and pictures taken from the collections of the Science Museum, the National Museum of Photography, Film and Television, and the National Railway Museum, hear about the stories behind many of them and enter into debates through a unique on-line resource.

10   **Scottish Network for Able Pupils** (http://www.ablepupils.com) is the youth section of the Scottish Network for Able Pupils (SNAP) site, specifically designed for young people to socialise, get advice, share life experiences and generally help each other out in the way that only other young people can. It also offers some links to other sites that able youngsters have found of interest.

11   **Scoilnet** (http://www.scoilnet.ie/) is an Internet initiative for Irish schools that is broadly similar in scope to the UK's National Grid for Learning.

12   **World InfoZone** (http://www.worldinfozone.com) provides links to news and information sites around the world, as well as a series of educational travel features, quizzes and photo galleries. The Linking the World section offers detailed information about selected countries, while the InfoZone provides links grouped by theme, such as art, history, music and sport.

13   **Xcalibre** (http://www.xcalibre.ac.uk/) is for the gifted and talented, providing links to many other websites that could be used by gifted pupils.

14   **G & T wise** (http://www2.teachernet.gov.uk/gat/) is for those looking for particular G&T materials. Browse the catalogue of resources by subject, key stage or teaching focus and/or use the search facility to find exactly what is required in the extensive database. Choose Quick or Advanced search, or use Quality Standards criteria.

CASE STUDY

Differentiation by e-mentoring

Heriot-Watt University Edinburgh: SCHOLAR Programme

'The Biggest E-Learning Programme in the World!'

http://www.scholar.hw.ac.uk   e-mail: info@scholar.hw.ac.uk

Heriot-Watt has an internationally renowned expertise in distance learning and computer-supported open learning, doing pioneering work in science, engineering, management and languages to educate the industrialists, professionals and thinkers of tomorrow.

The SCHOLAR programme, designed to improve student choice and flexibility, provides common educational resources and a 'virtual college' support network to help pupils progress between school, college and university. SCHOLAR was developed by Heriot-Watt University and is now distributed and delivered by the Interactive University. The programme was designed to provide extremely high-quality interactive materials for delivery over the Internet. Drawing on the University's special expertise in interactive and distance learning, SCHOLAR materials have been specially written by subject specialists from schools, colleges and the University. They bring together the best of innovative learning with tried-and-tested educational approaches, providing students with up-to-date knowledge and skills.

Subject mastery

Whatever pathway pupils choose, they gain a sound understanding of the subject they are studying using SCHOLAR materials that have been specially written for national programmes, using teams of subject specialists and reviewers from schools, colleges and the University.

Prospective students' pathway to careers in science and engineering

SCHOLAR can be the vehicle to a career in science or engineering. The SCHOLAR supported-learning programme gives pupils the flexibility to choose how far they go in their studies and how fast they progress. They can earn credits to gain exemptions

CONTINUED

from some university or college courses, meaning that they can progress faster towards a higher education degree. Because they can study at a time and place which suits them, the pupils are in control, being able to fit study around school and other commitments, or concentrate study over shorter periods. Guidance and support are always near at hand, through the local SCHOLAR school, college or university.

SCHOLAR provides on-line support for students taking science subjects at higher and advanced higher level and is available to all local education authority secondary schools in Scotland. The Heriot-Watt SCHOLAR Forum was established in May 2000 to deliver the Heriot-Watt SCHOLAR materials within the partner institutions. This is essentially a 'virtual college' to provide access to the on-line facilities complemented by local tutorial support provided by the teachers and lecturers within the participating institutions. The on-line facilities include:

- on-line texts with embedded activities and examples;
- automatically-marked formative assessments;
- simulations to promote understanding of more challenging areas;
- animations and visualisation to bring diagrams and equations to life;
- interactive tutorial exercises to develop and consolidate learning;
- on-line discussion groups which bring together learners and teachers;
- an on-line professional development forum where teachers can share their expertise and discuss issues;
- a sophisticated reporting system allowing pupils to monitor and reflect on their own progress;
- a teacher reporting system which allows teachers to see the class's work, compare it with the correct answer, comment on pupil answers and award a mark.

SCHOLAR local or SCHOLAR direct

Pupils can choose to study through a partner school or college in their area.

Registration

Pupils and teachers are registered through their institution's 'SCHOLAR Contact', who is typically a deputy head teacher or business manager. SCHOLAR does not take registrations directly from pupils or from subject teachers, and expects schools to manage their own pattern of SCHOLAR registrations. Partnership with the major school management information system providers allows this exchange of data to be effortless.

Each SCHOLAR Contact is supplied with briefing notes on how registration works, and the answers to many registration questions can be found in each institution's copy of the *SCHOLAR Navigation Guide*. There are also regular briefing meetings for school-based administrators.

SCHOLAR tutors and teachers

Tutor guides: A series of tutor guides is provided for the SCHOLAR courses. These cover the approach that has been taken to the curriculum in that subject, and give hints on how on-line activities and assessments might be used.

On-line reports: The e-learning environment stores information about pupils' activities and achievements, which is made available to accredited teachers within the pupil's own school, while pupils, of course, see only their own personal information.

This information can be an invaluable tool to teachers and pupils for monitoring progress and attainment and indicating the next steps.

SCHOLAR staff development: Staff development is a major part of the SCHOLAR activity, ensuring that teachers can log on and get started with the SCHOLAR programme. In addition to the teaching and learning materials and tools supplied by SCHOLAR, schools in partner local authorities are entitled to participate in a programme of continuing professional development designed to support and encourage the use of SCHOLAR and e-learning in general. The courses on offer address the pedagogic implications of on-line learning, issues specific to the successful implementation of the SCHOLAR resource, and utilisation of the ever-growing range of computerised tools available to support the 21st-century teacher. These opportunities are all free at point of use for educational staff in participating schools and authorities. Regional events mean that there is nearly always a venue within reasonable travelling distance, and video conferencing may be used where locations are remote from each other.

In Scotland, Heriot-Watt runs an annual 'SCHOLAR Conference' which provides an opportunity for teachers to meet up with other members of the SCHOLAR community and exchange examples of good practice.

About the Interactive University (IU)

The Interactive University was launched in October 2002 by Heriot-Watt University and Scottish Enterprise and extended to a number of partner universities. It is a market-led organisation specialising in the development and delivery of accredited e-learning programmes within the global post-compulsory education sector. The IU's primary objective is to become Scotland's centre of excellence in e-learning and the leading source of e-learning products and services, technology and research.

Gerry Toner, Heriot-Watt University's SCHOLAR Programme Director, said: *'The SCHOLAR Forum has the support of all the Local Education Authorities in Scotland and is available to all 40,000 secondary school pupils. This makes it the single largest e-learning forum in the world, which is a major achievement. It gives Scottish schools a significant lead in e-learning, putting them at the cutting edge in technology terms. No less significant, it gives school staff the opportunity to develop suitable pedagogies for the successful implementation of e-learning and develop their professional expertise.'*

The Pushkin Prizes

'The great thing about creative writing is, it's not like maths; there's not a right or a wrong way to do it ... the creative voice comes from inside you.'

Keith Gray, Judge 2004

The Pushkin Prizes (http://www.pushkinprizes.net) began when some of Alexander Pushkin's descendants, together with lovers of his work, gathered together in 1987 to mark the 150th anniversary of his death. Lady Butter, inspired to perpetuate her ancestor's memory in a unique and appropriate way, launched the creative writing competition as a pilot project in Scottish secondary schools in Tayside in 1988. The project was such a success that in 1992 a charitable trust was established, and since then the extent of the project has expanded to include every local authority secondary school in Scotland as well as schools in and around Pushkin's home town of St Petersburg. All pupils in the first two years of secondary education are eligible to enter the competition, and there is a special endeavour award available to those who receive additional support for their reading and writing.

The Prizes aim to encourage young people to gain insights into their own lives and the lives of other people through their writing. They offer young people the chance to meet peers from different cultures, establishing lasting friendships through an understanding of each other's lives and preoccupations. Prize-winners are invited to attend a residential creative writing course, where two professional writers provide seminars and individual tutorials designed to help them develop their writing.

The Scottish competition

Each pupil submits a folio of three pieces of original writing. Pupils can write about anything they choose – anything that sparks their interest, concern or passion. The work can be poetry, prose, drama or reportage, and can be written in English, Scots or Gaelic.

Prominent Scottish writers form a panel of judges (past members have included Anne Fine, Mollie Hunter, Joan Lingard, Magnus Linklater, Norman MacCaig and Edwin Morgan). They look for original, imaginative writing in any genre. Prize-winners are selected based on the breadth and consistency of the work in their folio.

The Russian competition

Alexander Pushkin (1799–1837) is Russia's greatest poet, as revered by Russians as Robert Burns is by Scots. Pushkin lived for some time in St Petersburg, a beautiful city that now has museums, statues and institutions dedicated to his memory. Nearly 30 schools in St Petersburg take part in the Pushkin Prizes. A panel of judges in Russia selects 12 of the best entries, and pupils translate their work into English for submission to the judges in Scotland. The Russian prize-winners travel to Scotland where they attend a creative writing course together with the Scottish winners.

The pupils are always eager to maintain links with each other; the recent ease of availability of e-mail and MSN in Russia means that contact between the winners from the two countries is pretty easy. The St Petersburg schools value contact with Scottish schools, and this is an effective way to introduce pupils to another country, its people and culture.

An annual anthology is published including some of the writing undertaken on the residential creative writing course, together with entries by a wide range of pupils from St Petersburg and all over Scotland. The anthologies are published by The Pushkin Prizes and are available via the website (www.pushkinprizes.net).

'The chances are I would not still be writing if it weren't for the Pushkin. At that kind of age it is easy to give up on hopes because they appear unachievable, so it is vital that young people are given encouragement when they show interest or talent in any field and even if they do not.'

This 13-year-old first prize winner went on to Glasgow University.

📖 FURTHER READING

Maker, C.J. (1982) *Curriculum Development for the Gifted.* Austin, TX: Pro-Ed

Teare, B. (1999) *Effective Resources for Able and Talented Children.* Stafford: Network Educational Press

Teare, B. (2001) *More Effective Resources for Able and Talented Children.* Stafford: Network Educational Press

USEFUL WEBSITES

International Baccalaureate Organisation:
http://www.internationalbaccalaureate.co.uk/
RM SuccessMaker Enterprise: http://www.rm.com/Secondary/Product.asp?cref=PD1068
RM Case Studies: http://www.rm.com/secondary/search/advancedsearch.asp?page=casestudies
http://www.ablepupils.com/
http://www.bbc.co.uk/learning/
http://www.bbc.co.uk/schools/
http://www.bbc.co.uk/schools/communities/onionstreet/
http://www.bbc.co.uk/schools/revision/
http://www.becta.org.uk/
http://www.carelpress.co.uk/quizpage.htm
http://www.curriculumonline.gov.uk/default.htm?cookie%5Ftest=1
http://www.enrichuk.net/
http://www.exscitec.com/
http://www.hoagiesgifted.org/
http://www.ngfl.gov.uk/
http://www.ngfl.gov.uk/what.jsp?sec=2&cat=265&clear=y
http://www.scholar.hw.ac.uk
http://www.scoilnet.ie/
http://www2.teachernet.gov.uk/gat/
http://www.worldinfozone.com
http://www.xcalibre.ac.uk/
http://www.pushkinprizes.net

Language Activity 3

For this activity, you will need access to an up-to-date English dictionary.

Exercise A

Use your reference source to explain the origin and current use of each of the following technical terms. You should write short, but detailed, paragraphs.

1. centrifugal
2. transistor
3. antibiotic
4. bleep
5. apartheid
6. coexistence

Exercise B

Expand the initials below and write a brief explanation of how they came to be in common use:

1. CSI
2. WMD
3. CID
4. MRSA
5. HIV
6. DNA
7. UNESCO
8. FIFA
9. IOC

Exercise C

Each of these foreign words or phrases has been adopted into the English language – identify the source language and match each term with the phrase that best fits its meaning.

1.	per capita	something causing excessive anxiety
2.	raison d'être	the good life
3.	ex officio	for one specific purpose
4.	la dolce vita	a thing already done
5.	locum tenens	a sudden decisive stroke in politics
6.	in camera	shared equally by all
7.	Deo volente	list of characters in a play
8.	tête-à-tête	by virtue of his office
9.	ad hoc	to the point of disgust
10.	bête noire	God willing
11.	ad nauseam	in secret
12.	fait accompli	purpose in life
13.	dramatis personae	my fault
14.	mea culpa	temporary replacement
15.	coup d'état	one to one

Rules about adding suffixes:

When a suffix begins with a vowel, the final consonant is doubled when there is **a single vowel** *before the last letter when the accent of the word is on the* **last** *syllable.*

Exceptions to this rule:

Some words where the accent is on the **first** *syllable still double the final consonant.*

Words which take suffixes like **-ish, -ism, -ist, -ise, -ize** *do* **not** *double the final consonant.*

Words that obey the rule	Words that break the rule
submitting	referred (accent on first syllable)
marshalled	counsellor (accent on first syllable)
rebellion	equalling (double vowel)
	cancellation (accent on first syllable)

Variations:

If the vowel before the last letter is **double,** *or the root word* **does not** *end in a single consonant, the final letter is* **not** *doubled. (an exception is wool – woollen)*

Words that obey the rule	Words that break the rule
coolest (double vowel)	symbolic (single vowel/consonant)
violently (double consonant)	civilian (single vowel/consonant)
blackmailer (double vowel)	

Note: Many of the words which **break** the rules in **UK English** use follow them in **US English** spelling – *e.g. equaling; woolen*

When undertaking research in order to answer a question or solve a problem, you may need to use a variety of resources.

Then you will have to communicate your findings effectively.

The following structure may be useful.

Step 1:　Make up lots of questions about your topic.
　　　　　Choose *one* question.
　　　　　Formulate one or more hypotheses about this question.

Step 2:　Review the literature/software to find out what is already known
　　　　　about the topic.
　　　　　Make notes – list references – select quotations – remembering
　　　　　details of the source and page numbers.
　　　　　DO NOT COPY (except for quotations).

Step 3:　Find a way to answer your question or to decide whether your
　　　　　hypothesis is true or not. Design a plan to do this.

Step 4:　Collect information according to the plan. Analyse this systematically.

Step 5:　Form a conclusion about your question or hypothesis based on the data you
　　　　　have analysed.

Step 6:　Present this conclusion in an appropriate way. You should include the evidence that
　　　　　led you to your conclusion and remember to include references and quotes.

　　　　　Your presentation may be written, graphic or pictorial or spoken.
　　　　　Choose the method which best suits your evidence. If you decide to do a
　　　　　spoken presentation, include visual aids and consider using Power Point.

Step 7:　If your research has raised additional questions, include these in
　　　　　your presentation.

Chapter 8

Enrichment

This chapter looks at

- Defining enrichment
- Schoolwide enrichment model (SEM)
- Enrichment activities embedded in the secondary curriculum
- 'Bolted-on' enrichment activities
- Enrichment by curriculum insert
- Enrichment for gifted and talented pupils
- E-learning websites
- Science after school
- Enrichment by design

Educational enrichment is '*the deliberate rounding out of the basic curriculum subjects with ideas and knowledge that enable a pupil to be aware of the wider context of a subject area.*' (Freeman, 1998)

DEFINING ENRICHMENT

There may be some confusion between the concepts of enrichment and extension; some use the terms interchangeably, considering both to refer to differentiation of the subject curriculum encompassing the exploration of a topic to a greater extent than is normally required; others think of extension work as being accelerated progress to more challenging subject content and concepts (Eyre, 1997), while enrichment is a wider context for learning extending into areas beyond the usual curriculum content. Yet another view is that enrichment activities are not directly linked to the curriculum but offer all pupils additional experiences that may, at best, enhance their learning or, at least, raise their awareness of life beyond the school environment.

SCHOOLWIDE ENRICHMENT MODEL

The schoolwide enrichment model (SEM) (Renzulli and Reis, 1985) is a plan for delivering curriculum enrichment and acceleration to all pupils, built on the success of programmes devised for the gifted and talented. In this model, schools develop their own enrichment programmes, offering general enrichment to groups of pupils while allowing individualisation of the curriculum for faster learners as well as opportunities for small groups and individuals to create and carry out investigations. The aim of this model is to raise the attainment of all pupils and address underachievement issues by integrating challenging and enjoyable high-end learning experiences into the curriculum, to create opportunities for pupils to apply knowledge to real-life situations, and for the gifted to engage in creative and practical thinking and problem finding as well as problem solving. This working framework, based on the provision of opportunities, resources and encouragement for all pupils to help them achieve their full potential, labels the provision, not the pupil, by providing opportunities to develop gifted behaviours rather than merely to identify them.

Three major components that make up the SEM (Renzulli and Richards (2004) are:

- The total talent portfolio (TTP), a profiling tool used to gather and record information about pupils' abilities, interests and learning styles, to inform decisions about curriculum modifications and enrichment activities.

- Techniques designed to assess pupils' mastery of curriculum content, adjust curriculum pace and content levels, and identify enrichment and acceleration opportunities for those who progress through the curriculum faster.

- Enrichment learning and teaching strategies that are integrated into the curriculum to ensure opportunities for high-end learning.

The SEM requires schools to take a flexible approach to differentiation of the curriculum to help teachers enhance the abilities of pupils by first assessing their strengths, and then devising enrichment opportunities and resources to develop these. The SEM model has been successful in addressing the problems of underachieving pupils, and it can also be used to suggest alternative learning pathways for those pupils who succeed in more traditional learning environments but are not effectively challenged.

ENRICHMENT ACTIVITIES EMBEDDED IN THE SECONDARY CURRICULUM

Many subject teachers respond to the different learning needs of their pupils by providing a learning environment designed to improve the attainment levels of all pupils by blending a differentiated curriculum with meaningful enrichment activities. Some of these are:

- competitions such as creative writing, the design of a poster or the invention of a useful classroom gadget;

- challenges, for example, a question or problem for the week at class, year or whole-school level;

- opportunities for collaboration giving pupils the chance to plan, select, analyse and discuss their own work;
- real-life problem-solving activities, from the subject curriculum or based on current events.

All pupils should have access to library and ICT resources, including software appropriate for extension and enrichment. There are many excellent websites available that not only support the regular subject curriculum but also offer a wide range of non-threatening enrichment opportunities to all pupils (see Enrichment by e-learning, pages 81–3).

Many schools – and governments – require that adults who work closely with pupils are carefully screened, and this process may deter teachers from bringing in outside experts to provide appropriate enrichment activities. Electronic contact, by video conferencing or e-mentoring, suitably supervised, may resolve this difficulty. The Scottish Enterprise E-mentoring Programme (Cadmuir Consultancy, 2003) provides an effective way of connecting secondary pupils with adult mentors, helping them to:

- develop ICT skills, encouraging the use of ICT across the curriculum and in real-life situations;

- link learning at school with skills for the world of work;

- motivate pupils to succeed;

- allow input into education from industry.

'BOLTED-ON' ENRICHMENT ACTIVITIES

Some enrichment is aimed at pupils who are interested in particular activities and opportunities, provided through:

- lunchtime and after-school clubs that offer opportunities for all interested pupils (see Science after School, pp. 84–5);

- study support activities offering a wider experience of learning activities;

- production of a school newspaper or magazine;

- inviting poets, writers, actors, sports personalities into school to provide positive role models;

- educational visits to cultural centres, museums and galleries, and to the theatre, concerts, sporting events;

- performance-related activities in sport, dance, drama, music.

ENRICHMENT BY CURRICULUM INSERT

Sometimes schools offer enrichment activities as part of the timetable (Renzulli, 2003), and a whole-year group may be timetabled together for 'enrichment'. Advantages in this model include the possibility of working with other local schools to share expertise, provide a peer group for similarly gifted pupils and increase the range of activities. However, a possible disadvantage for gifted pupils is the risk that, while offered generally enriching activities, they are not provided with any opportunities to explore and extend their specific abilities.

Sometimes gifted pupils who progress rapidly through the secondary curriculum take on the study of additional subjects that are not normally on offer to pupils at their level. These may be alternative classroom activities during subject tuition time, or squeezed into the existing curriculum, perhaps by giving time out from subjects where targets have already been achieved. However, the most enriching experiences for gifted pupils will be those that are firmly embedded in areas of specific ability.

ENRICHMENT FOR GIFTED AND TALENTED PUPILS

While general enrichment activities can enhance the learning experiences of gifted and talented pupils, they also need to have access to specially designed programmes that allow the inclusion of much more advanced content and processes (Teare, 1997). Unlike those provided through curriculum differentiation, these activities should not be open to all pupils and, though they should challenge gifted pupils to the point of failure, they should also provide a learning environment where it is emotionally safe to do so, by:

- using curriculum materials from later stages or higher levels of study as well as commercially and locally produced materials for gifted and talented pupils;

- entering eligible pupils for regional and national competitions;

- using the expertise and interests of older gifted and talented pupils to mentor younger pupils, providing them with appropriate role models;

- use of the Internet for independent research and distance learning;

- arranging mentoring by subject experts on a one-to-one basis, perhaps electronically (see Enrichment by out-of-school-hours activities, pp. 84–5);

- organising master classes or project work by experts in specific areas (see Enrichment by design, pp. 85–7);

- provision of demanding and challenging homework to develop study and research skills (see language homework programme, pp. 65–7).

E-learning is available to schools in a variety of ways, and may provide an excellent route to enrichment opportunities for gifted pupils in small or isolated schools. Where big city schools might be able to invite professional writers or musicians in to deliver master classes to gifted pupils, small or geographically remote schools may have to look for electronic solutions for enrichment activities. For example, the BBC *Get Writing* website offers on-line expert advice and structured courses and writers workshops. Stella Duffy, author of *Eating Cake* (1999) and *Immaculate Conceit* (2000), provides a whistle-stop guide for young writers to the process of finding their own personal writing style, including tips and exercises, a mailing list and details of writing competitions. While no substitute for a master class with a professional, this could provide valuable enrichment for an aspiring writer.

No matter which approach to enrichment a teacher chooses, it is clear that, while such activities should be available to all pupils, gifted and talented pupils often require different or enhanced provision.

ENRICHMENT BY E-LEARNING: SOME CURRICULAR WEBSITES

Few of these curricular websites are specifically for gifted and talented pupils, though most provide appropriately enriching activities. There are many curricular websites that can be easily found by following links, or in web portals such as those listed in Chapter 7.

1 **Active history** (http://www.activehistory.co.uk/) is packed with interactive simulations, educational arcade games and virtual interviews, as well as worksheets and lesson plans.

2 **Active Science**, GlaxoSmithKline (http://www.activescience-gsk.com/home.cfm?init=1) offers free on-line activities and downloadable information and worksheets:

- challenging games supported by downloadable databases for independent study;

- worksheets and information available for most topics;

- easy to use and yet thought-provoking;

- links to sites that may offer useful information.

3 **British Museum** (http://www.thebritishmuseum.ac.uk) contains information about the Museum's collection of antiquities from cultures around the world. The learning section provides details of resources and programmes for all ages offered by the Museum's education department. The Compass database allows users to search for images of selected objects, chosen to reflect the wide range of the Museum's collections.

4 **Chemistry and You** (http://www.chemistryandyou.org). By taking snapshots from the lives of five people around the world, shows how many of the things we take for granted would not exist without the chemical industry. The site also provides two interactive games, exploring the items found in a typical living room and supermarket.

5 **Children's Express (UK)** (http://www.childrens-express.org/) is a programme of learning through journalism for young people aged 8–18. Members in the United Kingdom regularly see their work in local and national newspapers, and hear each other on radio and television. They have published more than 700 stories, which can be read on this site.

6 **Cool Math** (http://www.coolmath.com/), this US mathematics site offers lots of maths activities for pupils aged 13 and older, with pages for parents and teachers and a wide range of entertaining maths and science games as well as links to similar sites.

7 **Eco Schools** (http://www.eco-schools.org.uk) is an environmental award programme for schools. Pupils are expected to be involved in all parts of the decision-making process and activities undertaken.

8 **Energy Quest** (http://www.energyquest.ca.gov/), from the California Energy Commission, contains information, puzzles, games and stories about energy, covering electricity production, issues of sustainability, tips on energy saving and ideas for science projects on energy.

9 **Foodlink** (http://www.foodlink.org.uk) contains on-line quizzes, downloadable resources and a directory of web links and 'The A-Z of Food Safety' and 'FactFiles' on all aspects of food safety in the home, focusing on hygiene, food storage, food preparation and food poisoning.

10 **Geography Exchange** (http://www.geography-site.co.uk/index.html) offers a wealth of geographical information, with pages covering aspects of physical geography.

11 **Global Footprints** (http://www.globalfootprints.org) offers information, interactive quizzes, resources and activities to help younger pupils take steps towards a more sustainable future by completing an on-line quiz to find out how big their global footprint is, and learn how to reduce it.

12 **ICT GCSE** (http://www.ictgcse.com) provides resources for pupils studying ICT for exams, including downloadable exercises, on-line quizzes and project guides on spreadsheets, word processing, databases and web design, as well as a series of animated movies on various topics.

13 **MapZone** (http://www.mapzone.co.uk/), created by Ordnance Survey, is an interactive website to help pupils develop mapping skills. 'Homework Help' includes activities, animations, games and quizzes on topics such as map symbols, grid references and compass directions, as well as printable resources and the downloadable MapBuilder tool.

14 **MathsNet** (http://www.mathsnet.net/) provides curriculum resources, on-line puzzles, news and articles to support mathematics teaching and learning.

15 **Mathszone** (http://www.mathszone.co.uk/) is a collection of links to free interactive resources on the Internet for teaching mathematics.

16 **Museum of Science and Industry in Manchester** (http://www.msim.org.uk) has an 'Exhibitions' section with audio and video clips relating to science, transport and power in the past, present and future. The 'Hands-on' section has interactive games on scientific themes, including sound and hot-air balloons.

17 **NASA's Educator Astronaut Program** (http://www.edspace.nasa.gov/) invites pupils to meet the men and women of NASA who explore space by going there. There's a lot more going on at NASA than just exploring space. Pupils can join the Earth Crew to become part of the NASA team, ride the Vomit Comet or spend a day underwater as a human submarine and go to Astronaut School! There is also an opportunity to find out about exciting careers at NASA.

18 **National Museums and Galleries of Wales (Amgueddfeydd ac Orielau Cenedlaethol Cymru)** (http://www.nmgw.ac.uk) provides information about the National Museum and Gallery of Wales in Cardiff, the Museum of Welsh Life, and Big Pit: The National Mining Museum. The education section offers interactive on-line games, downloadable resource packs and details of the education programme activities.

19 **NRICH Mathematics** (http://www.nrich.maths.org) project provides mathematical learning support for very able children of all ages, offering support, advice, in-service training to teachers and resources for mathematics clubs, including interactive games, problems, puzzles and articles.

20 **RealFrench.net** (http://www.realfrench.net) provides a collection of free French learning and teaching resources for exam pupils, developed by the Manchester Metropolitan University, with grammar notes, interactive exercises, on-line vocabulary games, a resource library, message boards, web links, worksheets and a verb conjugator.

21 **Sc1** (http://www.sc1.ac.uk), created by the Royal Society, the UK academy of science, for 16–19-year-olds, introduces some of the Royal Society's research scientists and the type of jobs they do, provides information about the latest scientific issues and debates, and features interactive games.

22 **Science On-line** (http://www.scienceonline.co.uk/) activities cover biology, physics and chemistry, and include instructions for pupils as well as teachers' notes and links to websites that illustrate scientific activities with text, images, audio and video, and are intended to improve the quality of lessons, with classroom activities that have been integrated with specific websites – including the BBC's Planets site and pages from sites in science departments at a number of universities in the United States.

23 **Solar System** (http://www.bbc.co.uk/science/space/solarsystem/index.shtml) explores the Sun, the planets, their moons, asteroids and comets:

  ● experience an amazing variety of worlds;

  ● run the gauntlet of floating rocks and boulders in the asteroid belt;

  ● encounter the icy comets that wander through the outer solar system;

  ● take a 3-D interactive tour of the solar system;

  ● access news, games and homework help on the planets.

24 **The Maths Challenges** (http://www.ukmt.org.uk/) are organised by the United Kingdom Mathematics Trust. These are national competitions and other mathematical enrichment activities for 11–18-year-old UK school pupils, and those who perform exceptionally well are invited to take part in follow-on rounds that require full, written mathematical solutions. Some pupils may be invited to attend the National Mathematics Summer School, based on their performance.

25 **The Scottish Seabird Centre** (http://www.seabird.org/) is an award-winning wildlife centre where visitors enjoy a close encounter with nature, with live webcams providing a glimpse of amazing wildlife.

26 **The Theatre Museum** (http://www.peopleplayuk.org.uk) site is based on the Theatre Museum's collections, and it aims to stimulate interest in and enjoyment of the performing arts.

27 **The Virtual Artroom** (http://www.virtualartroom.com) is a free illustrated resource to help art and design teachers embed ICT into teaching and learning, covering image manipulation, animation, interactive exercises, art presentations, whiteboard starters, digital video and project ideas.

28 **US Environmental Protection Agency – Acid Rain** (http://www.epa.gov/acidrain/) provides information about acid rain's causes and effects, how it is measured, and what is being done to solve the problem.

29 **Young Engineers** (http://www.youngeng.org/) can take older pupils interested in engineering or technology out of the classroom and into the real world.

CASE STUDY

Science after school

Enrichment by out-of-school-hours activities

A group of second-year high school pupils and an enthusiastic young teacher started up an after-school club specifically for gifted scientists. Following its success, every year a few second-year pupils, selected on the basis of performance in first-year science, teacher recommendation and self-nomination, are invited to attend this after-school science club. Although attendance is voluntary, once pupils have made a decision to join the club, they are encouraged to continue their commitment.

The science after-school (SAS) club aims to:

- provide an environment for gifted pupils to develop their ability by enrichment and extension beyond the limits of the science curriculum;
- guide pupil-directed projects, allowing them to maintain interest in science;
- develop and advance scientific skills as required by the pupil-directed projects;
- challenge and develop scientific opinions through research, reasoning and critical thinking;
- provide varied opportunities for the pupils to showcase their work;
- have fun.

By encouraging the pupils to undertake projects of their own choosing, either individually or in a group, SAS allows the participants to:

- set their own targets without the limitations of the curriculum;
- increase their depth and breadth of knowledge;
- improve their scientific skills and techniques;
- develop critical thinking skills;
- associate and work with other gifted individuals;
- explore areas of interest, enhancing motivation and preventing underachievement;
- have opportunities to meet working scientists and gain first-hand experience of the application of science;
- have fun.

SAS also has many benefits to the science department as it encourages motivated, gifted pupils to continue the study of the sciences and raises the profile of science in the school.

Pupils are encouraged to research, test or experiment with their own ideas. If ideas are suggested to them, they are encouraged to reject, change or develop them in any way they deem appropriate. The consultative process covers safety issues and available equipment, although pupils always try to think of ways around a problem. For example, one group wanted to investigate and make pyrotechnic rockets, so they negotiated a project that involved working out the best combination of factors that could be used to fire an Alka-Seltzer-powered 'pop rocket' the furthest distance. This led to investigations on how to control the timing of 'lift-off'.

Once a topic for investigation is agreed, pupils use a unique combination of tasks to aid discovery and improve knowledge and skills. A topic on dissection involved discussion about the ethics as well as how to go about this. It was finally agreed to:

CONTINUED

- research the history, the need for and alternatives to dissection;
- discuss ethics and consider others' opinions;
- take an individual ethical stance;
- carry out a sheep heart/lung dissection – ethics permitting;
- revisit personal ethical stance and opinion.

Activities have included attending student conferences, presenting projects to primary school pupils and having the satisfaction of improving on a piece of work or idea.

Each year there is a 'parents evening' that acts as a showcase to family, friends and guests, with popular adult vs. pupil competitions – some with surprising results.

The SAS project is a springboard to link pupils to mentors from commercial/academic areas outside school for activities such as work-shadowing, or provision of advice and encouragement to pupils working on advanced projects. The club allows gifted young scientists to develop at their own pace towards self-directed targets and goals that shift according to individual needs, encouraging pupils to follow their interests.

Pupil evaluations

'The activities we do are just right at challenging me since we picked them, we already picked how challenging they were.' –

'Science club is great because you can do any experiments you want, there is a nice atmosphere, lots of equipment/materials that you can use – it's fun and there are lots of outside school opportunities.' –

CASE STUDY

Enrichment by design

Fantasy Design

Fantasy Design 2003–2006 (http://www.fantasydesign.org/) was funded by EU Culture 2000 and co-ordinated by Design Museum of Helsinki (Finland) in collaboration with Design Museum Gent (Belgium), Norsk Form (Norway), The Lighthouse (Scotland) and the Hindholm Socialpedagogiske Seminarium (Denmark). The partners in the project are expert organisations: museums of design, design promotion agencies and a training institute.

Schoolchildren and young people as designers

A European-wide project, this initiative was set up to empower young people as designers, to introduce them to professional designers in the school setting, and to enable them to work as teams in order to invent new and exciting products. It promoted basic skills in design:

- problem solving;
- cultural thinking ;
- artistic expression;
- innovative attitude to work.

An awareness and appreciation of objects was encouraged, and an inter-disciplinary approach took into account historical, social and economic points of view.

Fantasy Design, a three-year design education project, consisted of workshops and lectures by professional designers in schools, the provision of teacher training and the development of teaching materials in partnership with professional designers and manufacturers, eventually leading to an international exhibition.

Coming up with an idea that is innovative is not always easy, and developing the idea, producing a model, development sheet and specification of materials to manufacturers is not something everyone knows how to do – which is why professional designers needed to be involved at the school level. Through exchange of information and pairing of designers with schools to work on design briefs for manufacturing, pupils were exposed to practical experience of how the design process works. Teachers had access to hands-on, continued professional development by working with designers, and designers acquired information about how the educational process operates in schools. This provision benefited all involved, and if developed further could have a positive impact on design education.

The activities were implemented in each participating country simultaneously, and the partners agreed to adopt the same methods:

- arranging school visits by designers;
- teaching of design to pupils and organising workshops;
- provision of educational materials on design;
- mounting an international touring exhibition of pupils' designs.

The Lighthouse, Scotland – a fantasy approach to design

Lesley Riddell, Education Manager, The Lighthouse, Scotland's centre for Architecture, Design and the City (based on her 2005 article in *Fantasy Design, Children and Young People as Designers*).

The Lighthouse education department aims to push educational boundaries, to raise awareness on the importance of good design, to work with all age groups and to encourage a *fantasy* approach. These aims were achieved in collaboration with the Fantasy Design project, which not only provided an opportunity to fulfil them, but also permitted inspirational experiences of working with gifted Scottish schoolchildren and designers alongside leading organisations in Europe.

In January 2004, the Lighthouse invited schools all over Scotland to participate in the Fantasy Design project. Young designers who already appeared to have the *fantasy* element in their design work and educational output were interviewed, and those finally selected showed exceptional talent for presenting the design process in exciting yet educationally challenging ways, thus placing learning and creativity on equal terms.

The process began with a designer going into a school and leading a whole-day educational workshop. A typical workshop (see p. 88) lasted one day and included all of the following stages:

- brainstorming;
- highlighting two main ideas;
- working the ideas through to a more focused product/concept;
- choosing a final idea and developing the aesthetic, technical and innovation elements of the product;

- designing the product development sheet to include all the design specifications;
- making a model that could represent the design three-dimensionally.

Once the product development sheet and the model were completed, these were submitted to the international jury in Helsinki who selected the finalists. The Lighthouse then undertook the task of trying to partner manufacturers with the pupil's designs in order to create professional prototypes for the travelling exhibition.

The young designer/makers involved in projects are the most powerful resources of the Lighthouse, so it was decided to embrace this strength and match designers to pupils whose work showed similar qualities. These designers were asked to make prototypes based on the specification sheets and models the pupils had produced, and to look at how they, as designers, could develop the ideas for manufacturing, thus adding a dimension beyond mere replication of the pupil's designs. It was anticipated that the prototypes, clearly developed from their own designs, would confirm that the pupils were capable of developing into professional designers, while also stressing the importance of design education.

The Fantasy Design project was not only successful in developing the skills and expertise of gifted young designers, it was also tremendous fun for all involved. The Lighthouse team worked with over 300 young people and teachers and professional designers from all over Scotland on this project, and the success of their collaboration is well illustrated by the enthusiasm and dedication of all involved and the quality of the final products shown in the international exhibition.

Workshop: Design a portable kitchen   Designer: Tassy Thomson

You are going on a mystery two-day journey and you need to carry all your own food and cooking equipment (clean drinking water will be available). In teams, design a mini food preparation and storage unit small enough for a young person (12 to 16) to carry or wear.

Final Product: 1:1 scale ergonomic prototype of a portable 'kitchen' in card or rubber.

Tasks:

- Image/texture/colour collage
- Simple line drawings of stacked and stored utensils
- Digital photography of meal preparation, portable containers and bags
- Group discussion about food preparation tasks
- Make 1:1 scale containers
  (3D shapes of different sizes – cubes/cylinders)
- Explore multi-functional surfaces or containers
- Join the containers together into an ergonomic 3D model for carrying
- Make annotated drawings of the 3D model
- Prototyping and testing

Materials: printed images; glue; paper; scissors; pens; utensils; A2 or flipchart paper; cardboard; plastics or fabric; tape; cable ties; foam; camera

Learning Objective:

To introduce students to life-size 3D product design based on the themes of food, nutrition, portability, ergonomics and sustainable sources of energy.

Learning Outcomes:

- Observation, through drawing and photography, of the tasks involved in cooking and storage of cooking utensils
- Analysing existing storage solutions in kitchens, camping equipment and in-transit food storage
- Exploring volume and space by making small folding cylinder and cube containers
- Discussion of materials' properties for creating the model including heat resistance, washable, lightweight, structural
- Exploration of sustainable types of fuel for heating or cooling
- Developing cardboard/foam and rubber prototypes of storage options for kitchen utensils and equipment

Teacher/Designer input:

- Images of existing models of camp stoves, 'chuck wagons' and kitchen storage solutions as well as rucksacks, trolleys, bags, yokes etc
- Samples of potential fabrication materials – aluminium, steel, rubber, plastics, wood resin coated textiles, foam etc, and information on their physical properties
- Templates for making boxes and cylinders in various sizes
- Examples of food containers such as egg boxes, fruit trays, fruit net bags, quick seal bags etc.

📖 FURTHER READING

Renzulli, J.S. (2003) *A Bird's Eye View of the Schoolwide Enrichment Model: A Practical Plan for Total School Improvement,* condensed executive summary from

Renzulli, J.S. (1997b) *Schools for Talent Development: A Practical Plan for Total School Improvement.* Mansfield Center, CT: Creative Learning Press, electronic version at http://www.gifted.uconn.edu/sem/semexec.html

Renzulli, J.S. (1998) *A Rising Tide Lifts All Ships: Developing the Gifts and Talents of All Students,* electronic version at http://www.gifted.uconn.edu/sem/semart03.html

USEFUL WEBSITES

BBC *Get Writing*: http://www.bbc.co.uk/dna/getwriting/

BBC *Develop Your Voice*: http://www.bbc.co.uk/dna/getwriting/module2p

Schoolwide Enrichment Model (SEM): http://www.gifted.uconn.edu/sempage.html

Van Tassel-Baska, J., *Basic Educational Options for Gifted Students in Schools*: http://cfge.wm.edu/documents/Basic_Educational_Options.htm

Becta – ICT Support Network: http://www.becta.org.uk/ictsn/

Hands-on Support: http://www.teachernet.gov.uk/wholeschool/ictis/ict_teaching/hos/

National Curriculum On-line: http://www.nc.uk.net

TeacherNet: http://www.teachernet.gov.uk

Virtual Teacher Centre (VTC): http://www.vtc.ngfl.gov.uk/docserver.php

http://www.activehistory.co.uk/

http://www.activescience-gsk.com/home.cfm?init=1

http://www.bbc.co.uk/science/space/solarsystem/index.shtml

http://www.chemistryandyou.org

http://www.childrens-express.org/

http://www.coolmath.com/

http://www.eco-schools.org.uk

http://www.edspace.nasa.gov/

http://www.energyquest.ca.gov/

http://www.epa.gov/acidrain/

http://www.foodlink.org.uk

http://www.geography-site.co.uk/index.html

http://www.globalfootprints.org

http://www.ictgcse.com

http://www.mapzone.co.uk/

http://www.mathsnet.net/

http://www.mathszone.co.uk/

http://www.msim.org.uk

http://www.nmgw.ac.uk

http://www.nrich.maths.org

http://www.peopleplayuk.org.uk

http://www.realfrench.net

http://www.sc1.ac.uk

http://www.scienceonline.co.uk/

http://www.seabird.org/

http://www.thebritishmuseum.ac.uk

http://www.ukmt.org.uk/

http://www.virtualartroom.com

http://www.youngeng.org/

Chapter 9

Acceleration

This chapter looks at:

- Deciding on acceleration
- Implications of acceleration
- Forms of acceleration
- Early entry
- Year skipping and concurrent studies
- Content and partial acceleration
- Benefits of acceleration
- Using full acceleration to resolve social and emotional difficulties of gifted children
- A primary/secondary cluster maths programme

Many believe that acceleration refers to the speed at which a pupil progresses through the school curriculum, while others believe it is the rate of a pupil's cognitive development, rather than an educational intervention (Van Tassel-Baska, 1992). These views are not necessarily contradictory – gifted pupils do demonstrate more rapid cognitive development than age peers and they do progress much more quickly through curriculum content. In most secondary schools, acceleration is a strategy that enables gifted and talented pupils to take part in learning experiences based on their performance in the curriculum, allowing progression in one or more subjects rapidly, working at a level well beyond their age/stage.

DECIDING ON ACCELERATION

Implementing an acceleration strategy may require changes in school organisation and adjustments to the structure of the timetable, often considered by school managers to be insurmountable obstacles, though actually irrelevant to pupils' progress. Secondary schools need to use flexible timetabling to provide gifted pupils with opportunities to reach a higher level of understanding and performance in the curriculum, and undertake more advanced studies and activities.

Full acceleration to a higher level could be seen by some as an 'easy' option for teachers (Colangelo et al., 2004) since it does not necessarily require curriculum adaptations, but it should not be offered lightly, and only when:

- a pupil has already met all the expected learning outcomes at the current level, would be near the top of the new class, and is motivated to work at a more advanced level;

- the teacher at the current stage finds it difficult to provide tuition and resources at the level required for continued progress, and lateral progression would not be enough;

- a pupil is at risk of underachieving or 'dumbing down' to operate at the same level as age peers, open to misinterpretation as laziness or lack of interest, perhaps involving negative behaviours;

- a pupil is socially and emotionally ready to progress.

Teachers should consider these questions before implementing an acceleration strategy:

1　Has the pupil's performance been compared across the curriculum with that of age peers and found to be considerably greater?

　　YES: The pupil may be a suitable candidate for acceleration.

　　NO: The pupil should probably not be considered for acceleration at this point, but teachers should investigate whether the pupil is underachieving, 'dumbing down' or whether there is any specific difficulty such as dyslexia that might impede progress. If underachievement is likely, strategies to reduce this should be implemented, and progress checked against the expected level of achievement after an appropriate interval.

2　Does the pupil already demonstrate significant achievement at the same level and/or in advance of those at the next age/stage?

　　YES: The pupil could be a candidate for acceleration; the extent of this to be determined by comparing the actual level of achievement with the learning outcomes expected in the destination group.

　　NO: The pupil should probably not be fully accelerated, but subject teachers should consider content acceleration and provide challenging enrichment activities.

3　Is the pupil's advanced level of achievement in a single subject only, or a group of subjects?

　　YES: Partial acceleration should be considered where the pupil joins an older group for only the subjects identified.

　　NO: Full acceleration may be the way forward.

IMPLICATIONS OF ACCELERATION

Any decision to promote a pupil permanently should involve consideration of the implications of this on the long-term educational experiences of the individual, in consultation with the pupil, parents, teachers and, if appropriate, an educational psychologist. Parental agreement and support are essential, but schools must ensure that all appropriate criteria have been met before opening discussion about acceleration, and should not agree to promote a pupil without supporting evidence. When the decision to accelerate has been taken, teachers of the new class must be fully informed of the ability and learning needs of the pupil, be ready to support integration into the group, and plan for gaps in general knowledge and personal experience.

Colangelo et al. (2004) identified 18 different forms of acceleration, falling into two broad categories; one where gifted pupils complete their education faster than their age peers, missing whole years; the other being individual subject acceleration where advanced content is encountered earlier than usual. This is the easiest strategy to implement, but has been criticised over the years as elitist, so, while being demonstrably the most effective form of provision for gifted pupils, it remains under-utilised. Gross (2004) attributes opposition to acceleration to a misconception that the social and emotional development of accelerated pupils may be at risk and gaps in their knowledge may slow them down, but points out that research has found that gifted pupils are at greater risk from inadequate intellectual challenge when kept with age peers than from being placed with older pupils.

Both high-achieving and underachieving pupils have been shown to benefit from acceleration (Gross and van Vliet, 2003), but schools must continue to ensure that each pupil considered for this is socially and emotionally ready. Some younger accelerated pupils need help to cope with the social and emotional demands of working with more mature pupils, though gifted pupils often appear to have little in common with age peers, preferring the company of older learners. Advanced ability to acquire and process information often leads gifted pupils to become familiar with ideas not usually encountered till a much later stage, leading to impaired communication with age peers, so their social and emotional development may be more closely related to mental rather than chronological age.

FORMS OF ACCELERATION

Van Tassel-Baska (1989) and Freeman (1998) agree that successful acceleration combines content acceleration to the level of the individual's abilities, planned enrichment and the opportunity to work closely with other gifted pupils. While acceleration may take various forms in the secondary school, it should always involve accelerated learning within the classroom. Acceleration may consist of:

● Early entry into a new phase of education, where a pupil enters secondary education before others of the same age, or early transfer to university; gifted pupils could miss a year or more of primary school to start the full secondary curriculum early, progress rapidly through the secondary curriculum and achieve university entry qualifications by age 15.

- Year group (grade) skipping involves promotion of pupils who are well advanced in several aspects of their curriculum above age peers by one or more years, differing from early entry since pupils could transfer to secondary school at the same time as age peers, but transfer into higher year groups than primary classmates. For pupils who demonstrate rapid progress across the secondary curriculum, missing a year or more is often considered the most appropriate way forward, even though it can necessitate extra tutoring for promoted pupils to 'catch up' with course content.

- Subject acceleration (content or partial acceleration) involves gifted pupils studying one subject at a more advanced level than age peers, or individuals joining more advanced groups in particular areas of the curriculum, effectively speeding up learning to match their demonstrated ability in the subject.

- Concurrent studies involves pupils remaining with age peers but following a more advanced course. This is common with bilingual pupils, who need to do more advanced work in their home language but are not ready to join an older group.

- Self- or teacher-organised studies is a form of curriculum differentiation that permits pupils to work at a more advanced level and may involve curriculum compacting, where only new work is covered, allowing gifted pupils to proceed at a much faster pace, in greater depth.

- Mentoring involves individual pupils working with an 'expert' in the subject concerned, perhaps an older pupil, a teacher, a visiting specialist or a university department, often incorporating curriculum compacting and enrichment.

- Specialist schools or units provide appropriate tuition for pupils who have been identified as having similar gifts who may need to work in groups as required for team sports and performing arts.

EARLY ENTRY

Transfer to the secondary school early requires close contact between primary and secondary teachers to follow specific guidelines both for preparing pupils for early entry to secondary school and to prepare secondary staff for the possible arrival of very young pupils. Because the pupils concerned may be very young, teachers often have concerns about physical and emotional maturity. Although younger pupils may be physically smaller than most secondary-age pupils, with less developed motor skills, lack of physical maturity should not be a particular obstacle despite potential difficulties in practical subjects where physical strength and motor co-ordination are required. While a 9-year-old might find it difficult to participate in team sports with 12-year-olds, and lack of height and reach could make access to workstations difficult, it is not uncommon for very small, physically immature children to be in classes with age peers, so secondary schools are often already prepared to anticipate problems linked to delayed motor development. Equally, some younger children are as mature physically as much older pupils, so parents and teachers should not consider size as a barrier to proposed acceleration.

Despite the findings of Gross (2004) and Colangelo et al. (2004) that accelerated pupils consistently achieve at a higher level and that gifted children often prefer to associate with older learners or adults, many parents and teachers still consider a possible lack of emotional maturity as a barrier to early entry to the secondary school.

Some gifted pupils who have achieved university entrance requirements at age 14 or 15 may not be ready to transfer to the tertiary stage, since their youth could bar them from many student activities, leading to increased isolation. Accelerated pupils may benefit from broadening their studies without compromising university entrance standards; others may take advantage of a structured gap year activity, such as a foreign exchange. Each case must be considered on its own merits in order to achieve the most appropriate provision for each individual concerned.

YEAR SKIPPING AND CONCURRENT STUDIES

One possible solution to opposition to early entry to secondary school is a combination of grade skipping and concurrent studies that allows gifted pupils to remain with age peers at primary school when motor co-ordination and emotional maturity are still developing, while studying secondary curriculum content. This strategy requires secondary subject and primary class teachers to work closely together, and time for this can be difficult to find. Taking this approach could allow gifted pupils to transfer into higher secondary year groups, determined by progress in their concurrent studies, though teachers would need to make provision to fill gaps in subject knowledge and experience. With appropriate support in place, gifted pupils can catch up very quickly, sometimes overtaking pupils in the new group, though secondary teachers need to remain aware that emotional immaturity may emerge in some areas and be ready to offer support as required.

CONTENT AND PARTIAL ACCELERATION

When gifted pupils demonstrate considerable ability in one or more subject areas at primary school, content acceleration may be easily organised since the timetable may be flexible enough to allow pupils from several stages to work together as a group, though actual delivery of subject content at an accelerated rate might be more difficult. Content acceleration is often part of differentiation and enrichment strategies, but these are not enough for some gifted pupils who need to be more thoroughly challenged and stretched by working with others of similar ability in a subject, but restrictions of the secondary timetable could make implementing a programme of partial acceleration very difficult. To arrange for accelerated pupils to attend subject classes at the required level, aspects of the timetable might have to be adjusted; the time when pupils are timetabled to attend subject classes and the time that the advanced subject class is taught. In order to attend subject lessons with an older group, a pupil will have to miss lessons in other subjects and be expected to catch up with the work, either at home or during 'gap' times when age peers are attending classes in the accelerated subject. Care would be needed to ensure that arrangements are in place for extra teacher input if pupils miss essential activities that could impair progress. Support at home is very important when partial acceleration is considered, and parents might be expected to help the pupil to catch up with aspects of the curriculum that had been affected by the demands of this provision.

Whatever decision is reached about the flexible use of time 'created' by adjusting the timetable of a gifted pupil, the process will work best if teachers take a positive approach, looking on the situation as an opportunity to improve provision and enhance the pupil's curriculum. This will make the pupil's learning experiences ultimately more effective and is likely to be more rewarding for the teachers involved.

BENEFITS OF ACCELERATION

Flexible implementation of various forms of acceleration enables gifted pupils to cover a range of subjects in greater depth and enrich their curriculum by:

- linking to a university department in order to take study to a more advanced level, by e-learning or by attending lectures;

- undertaking a thematic study;

- electing to take an extra subject, perhaps one not normally offered in the school;

- taking time out to do a school exchange abroad to provide a 'gap year' experience instead of transferring to university early.

CASE STUDY

Using full acceleration to resolve social and emotional difficulties of gifted children

Gifted children who start primary school already able to read fluently will try to fit in with age peers and join in their activities, but are often unable to do so. They may feel different from the other children and think they must be doing something wrong. This can lead to them becoming bored, angry, disobedient and frustrated, perhaps developing challenging behaviour at home and having difficulty accepting limits. Sometimes an educational or clinical psychologist may be asked to assess the child's 'difficulties'.

If cognitive assessments are carried out, such pupils are often found to be able to read well beyond their age and their verbal abilities are likely to be in the exceptionally high range. Performance abilities, too, are likely to be well above average, and there may be significant strengths in information handling, arithmetic skills and logical abstract thinking. However, some of these young gifted children may give up easily when faced with challenge or difficulty, despite their intellectual competence – they may believe that their responses must be 'perfect' and become anxious if they 'fail'. Even with frequent reassurances that they are not 'failing', some gifted pupils continue to perceive that they are, and this may lead to increased troubled behaviour, sometimes even to depression.

If gifted pupils are given the same teaching input and expected to perform at the same level as their age peers, this may accentuate difficulties in developing peer relationships and lack of faith in the teacher, as they may see no point in doing age-appropriate work that is too easy. Many may deliberately underachieve in an attempt to win acceptance from teachers and age peers (Gross, 2004: 17, 1989), but some are unable to compromise, becoming isolated and difficult, preferring to invent solitary intellectual stimuli. Gross (1998) describes some of the measures taken by gifted youngsters to prevent their classmates – and teachers – from discovering their true abilities. These 'screens of camouflage' range from the development of 'an alternative identity' achieving success in what is thought to be a more acceptable area such as music or sport, to deliberate concealment of giftedness in the classroom.

CONTINUED

If they are not challenged academically, and are experiencing failure in forming relationships, some gifted pupils may refuse to co-operate in class and be reluctant to engage in appropriately challenging tasks. Gifted children can develop low self-esteem if they have little access to other gifted young people who share their abilities and interests.

Provision to meet their needs in school must be sufficiently challenging. Boredom will quickly follow when the reward for finishing the set work and getting everything right is more of the same, at the same level. Quantitative differentiation that does not offer any opportunity for the study of more advanced content, involving higher order skills and advanced performance, only puts off boredom for a while.

Some gifted pupils can continue to experience problems relating to age peers, and may become increasingly unhappy and socially isolated, persistently underachieving by setting themselves the same standards as their classmates, and producing careless or incomplete work. They may be unco-operative, reluctant to do anything they find 'too easy' and refuse to do homework.

While acceleration to the next year group can lead to improvement on previous experiences, some pupils may still not be appropriately challenged, and teachers may not provide appropriate curriculum content if a gifted pupil is still not placed with other pupils of a similar ability level.

Some of these exceptionally able pupils may suffer from being held back and kept in age peer groups. If lateral extension of the primary school curriculum cannot meet the needs of gifted pupils and there is no actual peer group for them, they may have to be accelerated in order to be provided with a base from which to reach their educational potential. Provided that parents and teachers agree that a pupil is ready socially and emotionally, the best way forward may be early transfer to secondary school.

Before early entry to secondary school, it is important that an actual intellectual peer group is identified for the pupil concerned. Secondary subject teachers will expect accelerated pupils to perform at the same level as the rest of the class, even if there is evidence that they have already surpassed them academically. Placing an accelerated pupil in the first year of secondary may not always be appropriate and, once the novelty of the changed educational setting has passed, this may result in renewed boredom, lack of co-operation in school and behavioural difficulties. If it is to be an effective strategy for meeting the needs of exceptionally gifted pupils, acceleration must be to the correct level, where pupils can relate to an intellectual peer group. Many teachers will question a decision to place an 11-year-old in a class of 14-year-olds and raise many, often valid, objections. Each proposed acceleration must be dealt with on its own merits and decisions taken that are in the best interests of the pupil concerned. While it is important that teachers are informed and involved in any decision to accelerate a pupil at the time of transfer, other pupils do not need to know. In many cases, though pupils may may speculate about the age of a new classmate, after a short time differences are usually forgotten.

Once the decision to accelerate has been taken, schools should make arrangements for individual tuition for newly accelerated pupils to fill any gaps in subject knowledge and experience – similar to what is often routinely offered to pupils who enrol in the middle of the school year. With appropriate support and advance warning that they may need help with aspects of the course, even greatly accelerated pupils are able to face failure and take steps to overcome it.

CONTINUED

Parents and teachers to are often concerned about lack of social maturity, and this is frequently the major obstacle to acceleration of gifted pupils. While it is true that social immaturities are often apparent in the first few weeks, these should be considered to be part of the transition process and they usually disappear quite rapidly as the pupils concerned settle in and find their intellectual level in the new class. By the start of the next school year, most accelerated pupils appear to be at much the same social and emotional level as their classmates, any potential socio-emotional problems of gifted pupils being resolved once they are accelerated to an appropriate level.

CASE STUDY

Primary/secondary cluster maths programme

In June 1999, the head teacher of a secondary school expressed concern when research showed that less than 40 per cent of new material is introduced in maths each year from primary 6 to secondary 3. This pace was considered too slow for some able mathematicians, and it was thought that many could be underachieving, since exceptional mathematical ability might not be identified unless appropriate challenge was provided. It was decided that the high school needed to make provision to enable pupils to move through the maths curriculum in greater depth and at a more appropriate pace.

After exploring various options, senior managers decided that it would be best to start this programme at the primary 6 stage, and associated primary head teachers were approached about setting up a pilot programme. Extra staffing was put into the school's maths department, so that teachers could develop suitable materials and to enable links with local primaries to be formed in order to identify those gifted pupils whose maths was well ahead of that of the rest of their class.

Since pupils identified would benefit from specialist maths tuition, a weekly 'master class' was proposed, to be taught at the high school by specialist maths staff. Eligible pupils from cluster primary schools would attend this class for one afternoon a week for specialist maths teaching appropriate to their ability. Work would be set for completion in primary school maths time, and marking schemes and 'help' sheets were prepared for each primary teacher whose pupils were involved. The pupils would work only on *new* material, starting at appropriate levels and proceeding through a compacted maths curriculum at an accelerated rate, with some provision of enrichment activities designed to give pupils time to reflect upon and consolidate their learning.

Pupils participating in this programme would be placed in the same maths set on transfer to secondary school in order to continue their programme as a group.

The pilot proved very successful with the parents, teachers and pupils involved. This programme is now well established and has been emulated by several other primary/secondary school clusters.

CONTINUED

The accelerated maths programme

Stage 1: Primary staff identify gifted maths pupils and arrange for them to be taught in ability groups. Advice and materials (including assessment materials) provided by the high school maths department. Parents consulted about the implications of the programme.

Stage 2: Secondary maths staff visit primaries, meet with teachers and pupils and discuss testing for placement on the accelerated programme to be carried out by the high school maths staff.

Stage 3: All pupils reaching the required standard are offered places on the programme to be provided by the high school. There could be more than one group, since all eligible pupils to be offered places.

Stage 4: Pupils attend the high school for one afternoon a week to be taught by specialist maths teachers. Additional work is set at these sessions to be done in primary school groups during the week, and a homework programme is issued. Maths teacher monitors pupils' progress and arrange to visit the primary schools involved on a regular basis to maintain contact with primary staff. Some pupils find the demands of this course too rigorous, and may drop out. They would continue to work in top primary maths groups on appropriate content, but concentrate on 'broadening and deepening' (McClure, 2001) their skills.

Stage 5: On transfer to secondary school, pupils on the accelerated programme are put in the same class for maths, which becomes an accelerated group following a compacted curriculum, with all pupils doing more advanced work than age peers with advanced targets and closely linked to the national examination curriculum. A parallel group of gifted pupils is not accelerated, but pupils are capable of learning more advanced content at a deeper level, so a different course was devised for them, incorporating more enrichment activities.

Stage 6: Early presentation in maths exams with top results anticipated. Alternatively, pupils complete the examination course work and start the Higher curriculum without any 'break', actually taking examinations at the 'normal' time without interrupting the flow of their learning.

Stage 7: Pupils take examinations at Higher and Advanced Higher early, with the expectation of A passes.

This provision allows pupils gifted in maths to progress at an appropriate pace, according to their ability, to work with other similarly gifted pupils and to progress side by side, as individuals or as members of a group.

📖 FURTHER READING

Colangelo, N., Assouline, S. and Gross, M.U.M. (2004) *A Nation Deceived: How Schools Hold Back America's Brightest Students.* The Templeton National Report on Acceleration. Iowa City, IA: The University of Iowa. Electronic version at http://www.nationdeceived.org/

Wang, M.C., Reynolds, M.C. and Walberg, H.J. (eds), *Handbook of Special Education: Research and Practice*, Vol. 4. Oxford: Pergamon.

Chapter 10

Specialist Provision

This chapter looks at:

- Specialist schools
- Academies
- Talent searches
- Summer programmes
- Special programmes
- The World Class Arena initiative
- The City of Edinburgh Music School

All secondary schools provide specialist teaching across the whole curriculum. But sometimes even the skilled subject specialist is unable to provide tuition at the required level for gifted pupils, so visiting tutors may be brought in to meet their needs. While this is common in subjects like music and sport where expert tuition is needed in order to ensure that gifted and talented individuals have access to specialised training and support, it should also be possible in other areas of the curriculum, according to pupils' needs.

Sometimes specialist provision is offered as enrichment to pupils in groups, perhaps by inviting professional writers or performers to deliver master classes for those who have demonstrated giftedness in creative writing or acting. Sometimes specialists work with gifted pupils individually in order to help develop specific abilities, finding time for this by extracting pupils from either the subject concerned or from another part of the curriculum. Although this might cause timetabling difficulties, teachers would determine which option best meets the needs identified; more subject time might benefit a pupil, so specialist tutoring should be in addition to the subject curriculum already provided; or a pupil may be so far advanced in the subject that attending the usual class is no longer appropriate, and the specialist teacher would provide alternative lessons. Some gifted pupils might access specialist tuition electronically, using specially developed resources like World Class Tests that have been designed to meet the needs of gifted pupils, and can challenge and extend their abilities.

Individualising the curriculum in order to arrange specialist teaching for gifted and talented pupils may be complicated to organise, but it is possible, provided that there has been careful forward planning and the implementation is articulated to the timetabling framework of the school.

SPECIALIST SCHOOLS

Specialist secondary schools for gifted and talented pupils are often privately funded, either charging fees or requiring sponsorship. While all schools must teach a broad and balanced curriculum, specialist schools target a very narrow range of abilities in subjects such as performing arts, and they may find it difficult to provide a high quality general education as well as enriched learning opportunities for pupils in their specialist subject area. In a state-funded educational system, separate provision for gifted pupils could be perceived as unreasonable public expenditure and be open to accusations of elitism.

In Scotland there are government-funded national centres for dance, music, sports and languages, consisting of three specialist music schools, a specialist dance and musical theatre school, a sports academy and an international language school. These have been located within mainstream schools where pupils follow a flexible mainstream curriculum as well as having specialist tuition to develop their specific abilities and skills. Admission is open to all school-age pupils by audition, where panels consist of professionals in the field, and there are no general academic requirements for entry. The rationale for this provision is that pupils who are gifted in languages, sports or music often require tuition beyond what is normally available in schools, and dance and musical theatre are areas of expertise that would not normally be found in the school curriculum.

Policy for gifted education in England is inclusive, with a variety of approaches designed to integrate pupils with age peers as much as possible. This approach builds on general education, rather than viewing provision for the gifted as something extra, but it does not assume that all provision for gifted pupils will be in the mainstream classroom or school. If gifted pupils need access to specialist provision, then it should be made available, since lack of this could impede progress and attainment. Specialist schools and city academies are in place to expand the range of opportunities offered to gifted and talented pupils through the general school system. The National Academy for Gifted and Talented Youth (NAGTY) plays a leading role in the creation of opportunities and for specialist tuition.

The English Specialist Schools Trust supports a network of innovative, high-performing secondary schools in partnership with business and the wider community.

While this programme is not specifically for gifted and talented pupils, their mainstream classroom provision is enhanced by additional opportunities offered within and outside school in the arts, business and enterprise, engineering, the humanities, languages, mathematics and computing, music, science, sports or technology.

ACADEMIES

Renzulli's (2000) Academies of Inquiry and Talent Development (AITD) are not gifted programmes, but provide all pupils with opportunities, resources and encouragement to apply their interests, knowledge, thinking skills, creative ideas and task commitment to problems that they have identified themselves in the area they have elected to study. Like the English Specialist schools, possible academies might include:

- literature, languages, arts and the humanities

- applied mathematics

- social sciences

- fine and performing arts

- physical and life sciences

- sport and leisure studies

- computer science and technology.

Activities are directed towards the acquisition and application of advanced content and processes within each field of study, and pupils might progress through three stages of enrichment from general awareness-raising through planned development of specific skills to the investigation of specific problems or creative challenges.

City Academies are independent state-funded schools, sponsored by industry, foundations and other donors, that aim to improve standards and provide choice and diversity in socially disadvantaged areas for all pupils. These schools specialise in one or more subjects as well as delivering the national curriculum, and a range of specialisms offer curriculum-based enrichment activities that will provide support and challenge to gifted pupils.

NAGTY, launched in 2002, is based at Warwick University and is intended to:

- develop, implement, promote and support educational opportunities for gifted and talented young people;

- provide access for pupils to the formal and informal learning opportunities they need to help them convert their potential into high achievement;

- provide a nationally and internationally recognised centre to lead, support and inform the work of teachers and education professionals working to improve gifted and talented education in England.

Members of NAGTY benefit from access to a range of courses, with ICT services that help them to develop their potential further. Through the Student Academy, members become part of a gifted community and can take part in:

- short courses delivered by experts at locations across the country;

- Summer Schools providing in-depth focus on one subject in a university environment;

- academic study groups, offering e-learning guided by specialists;

- on-line forums where members discuss wide-ranging topics.

The Center for Talented Youth at Johns Hopkins University (CTY) offers educational programmes for pupils of exceptionally high academic ability by:

- offering challenging educational opportunities that develop the intellect, encourage achievement and nurture social development;

- developing best practices in educating highly able children;

- supporting teachers in their efforts to meet the needs of highly able students.

Stanford University's Education Program for Gifted Youth (EPGY) is dedicated to developing and offering multimedia computer-based distance-learning courses, combining technical and instructional expertise for high-ability students in a variety of subjects. In 2005, over 3,000 students from 28 countries were enrolled in EPGY.

The Irish Centre for Talented Youth (CTYI) works with young people of exceptional academic ability who have been acknowledged by the Irish Department of Education as having 'special educational needs'. The Centre aims to address these needs by:

- identifying high-ability pupils through annual talent searches;

- providing services for these pupils, including Saturday classes, residential summer programmes, correspondence courses and discovery days;

- giving support to parents and teachers;

- carrying out research.

TALENT SEARCHES

The CTYI talent search is designed to identify, assess, recognise and provide educational opportunities for mathematically and/or verbally talented secondary school pupils through:

- the opportunity to take the scholastic aptitude test (SAT), an excellent indicator of mathematical and verbal reasoning ability;

- invitations to take part in CTYI summer academic programmes should they reach certain standards on the SAT;

- the opportunity to qualify for a scholarship towards the cost of a CTYI summer programme at Dublin City University;

- gaining a certificate of participation from Dublin City University;

- invitations to annual discovery days which explore challenging topics.

The talent search programme implemented by the Australian Institute of Sport (AIS) in co-operation with state and territory institutes, academies of sport and national and state sporting organisations is a national, co-ordinated effort to search for sporting talent in Australia's young people. The Queensland Academy of Sport and The Central Coast Academy of Sport, New South Wales are local initiatives aimed at identifying and supporting elite and developing athletes as they strive for excellence within their sport, and might be the first step taken by gifted young athletes as they progress towards national and international competition.

CTY at Johns Hopkins University conducts the United States' oldest and most extensive university-based talent search for highly able youth. Since the first CTY talent search in 1972, designed to identify, challenge and reward academically able young people, CTY has expanded to offer a wide range of academic opportunities. In 2000, more than 90,000 students participated in the talent search and by 2005 it had identified nearly one million students and served over 100,000 students through its programmes.

SUMMER PROGRAMMES

The majority of summer experiences are designed to

- provide gifted pupils the chance to be with peers who share their skill level;
- create bonds between youth from around the country/world.

The chance to work with experts who are leaders in their chosen field gives pupils opportunities to stretch themselves and to expand their chosen areas of knowledge. Summer schools also offer social programmes in the evenings and at weekends with sporting, social, artistic and academic activities, including trips to the theatre, talent shows, international evenings and competitions. One exception is the City of Edinburgh Gifted and Talented Summer Programme, which offers small-scale, non-residential, free local provision to selected 12-year-olds.

NAGTY summer schools are residential courses that take place at eight higher education institutions throughout England and at Johns Hopkins University CTY in the United States. Courses last for two or three weeks, and pupils study a single course from a wide range, covering the arts, sciences and humanities. The Imperial College, London offers a full range of subjects across the sciences.

CTY Summer Academic Programs are three-week residential and day programmes offered through Johns Hopkins at 19 sites across the United States. EPGY Summer Institutes are three- and five-week residential summer programmes for academically talented and motivated high-school pupils at the Stanford University campus. Both are designed to enrich and accelerate academic pursuits and to share this experience with others who have similar interests and abilities. Courses are taught by Stanford instructors in mathematics, science, writing, humanities, computer science, engineering and music, covering topics not typically presented in high school.

Many universities and colleges offer short courses to prospective students. The Edinburgh College of Art Portfolio Preparation for Schools (PoPS) programme is an intensive, week-long experience available in architecture, studio-based drawing, painting and mixed media and sculpture with mixed media construction, with information sessions offered on portfolio requirements, including advice on presentation of the portfolio as well as on adding a 'design' element to an application portfolio.

SPECIAL PROGRAMMES

Distance e-courses may offer multimedia lectures that capture the informal nature of classroom instruction, while preserving a level of rigour appropriate to the subject matter. Stanford University's EPGY offers real-time virtual classroom sessions in which pupils and tutors interact using voice and shared whiteboard conferencing software to create a real-time interactive version of the lecture environment, providing a robust electronic forum in which pupils can interact. CTY at Johns Hopkins offers academically challenging distance education courses in writing, mathematics, computer science and physics, as well as 'live' programmes at college, university, science centre and museum sites around the United States.

There are many other special programmes offered by universities and colleges to older secondary-school pupils who are about to specialise in school subjects prior to moving to higher education. These programmes may be a combination of courses offered during school holidays, distance and e-learning opportunities, mentoring, lectures or links with those already taking various higher education courses.

All pupils who demonstrate giftedness in specific aspects of the curriculum – or in extra-curricular activities – may need tuition and support that is beyond the level of expertise of the usual subject staff of the school, and additional specialist help should be provided to ensure that this is available to them. Often suitably qualified specialists are not readily available, either in person or electronically, in which case biographies and autobiographies are useful alternatives in providing role models, especially for gifted pupils who are underachieving or disabled, by illustrating how even prominent or successful people experience triumphs, failures and hardships throughout their lives.

CASE STUDY

World Class Arena: Specialist subject provision for gifted and talented pupils

World Class Arena (http://www.worldclassarena.org)

World Class Arena is an international initiative devised by the British government's Department for Education and Skills (DfES) to identify and assess gifted and talented students around the world. World Class Arena items have been trialled by teachers and students in the United Kingdom, Australia, New Zealand and the United States. It offers World Class Tests in mathematics and problem solving and research, classroom support materials and resources for everyone involved in gifted and talented education.

World Class Tests

World Class Tests of problem solving and mathematics aimed at the top performers in the upper primary and lower secondary age groups were developed jointly by examiners in Britain, the United States, Australia, New Zealand and Hong Kong to help to identify and challenge pupils at the top 10 per cent ability range. Each

CONTINUED

test requires the application of creative thinking and logic to respond to problems and clear communication of thought processes. Each test has a paper and a computer component. To gain certification at pass, merit or distinction, pupils must take both components. Three grades are available.

Pupils can take World Class Tests in either problem solving or mathematics, or both. The problem-solving questions use contexts drawn from science, design technology, and mathematics, but require high level problem-solving skills rather than subject knowledge. While pupils do not need to have followed a specific curriculum for the problem-solving test, they need some prior knowledge for the mathematics test, and need to be able to apply this to new situations, using deductive reasoning to solve unfamiliar problems.

Pupils taking World Class Tests should be given specialist tuition using the specially designed classroom support materials and resources, and be able to:

- think creatively and logically;
- use thinking skills to solve problems and answer questions on subjects that they may not have studied;
- work out and respond to unfamiliar information;
- demonstrate clearly how they solve questions.

CASE STUDY

The City of Edinburgh Music School http://www.edinburghmusicschool.co.uk

The City of Education Council (CEC) Music School was established as a national centre of excellence combining integrated educational opportunities of the highest quality with the best possible intensive musical tuition. The young musicians who attend the school are probably their own best public relations organisation. Their public performances never fail to win admiration for their professionalism and exceptionally high standards. Their reputation and that of the CEC Music School continues to grow.

A preliminary audition is arranged through the Director of the Music School at any time during the academic year. On the basis of this informal meeting, advice is given on whether or not to proceed further. Those short-listed for a final audition are called in February, March or April for assessment by a panel of highly-renowned musicians. All instruments and all styles of music are considered equally. Over the years students have successfully secured places in the Music School with their performances on a wide variety of instruments such as drum kit, electric guitar, bagpipes and recorder, along with standard orchestral instruments. The audition is a straightforward 15-minute performance of music of the candidate's own choice, plus a variety of other possibilities such as aural tests, scales, sight-reading and improvising as appropriate. The whole audition normally lasts 30 minutes. The panel is aware of the widely differing backgrounds of the applicants and looks much more for potential ability than for present attainment. For this reason it is not possible to prescribe a level of performance required for entry at any stage, but it would be unrealistic to consider seriously a 16-year-old who was not already well on the way to the technical accomplishment expected by one of the major colleges of music. The City of Edinburgh Council offers places only to those pupils who, in the opinion of the panel, have a musical talent and personal

CONTINUED

motivation of such a degree as to justify a highly-specialised form of education. There are many musical children for whom a specialist education is not necessarily the best course.

Pupils are enrolled at a local high school and offered a flexible mainstream curriculum in consultation with pupils and parents; time for specialist music is created by extraction from selected subjects either wholly or partially for a year. One pupil may, for example, be extracted completely from geography for one year or attend only one out of two art lessons in the week. The curriculum is negotiable and no two Music School timetables will be the same. The aim is to set aside approximately a quarter of the school week for music, including all individual and small-group tuition. Much practice and all ensemble rehearsals take place outside the normal school day. There is a good deal of variation in the time allocation for music at this stage, according to the career intentions of the individual student. A normal pattern for a student aged 16 would be to sit Advanced Level music plus two other subjects. By sixth year, a well-qualified student, intent upon a music course beyond school, could be spending 50 per cent or more of the school week studying music.

All music students tend to get involved in music-making out of school as well as in school. They are expected to take part in the network of ensembles within the City of Edinburgh and beyond.

The intensive training – involving regular practice, various ensembles and individual expert tuition from the most talented and dedicated teachers in the land – paves the way for pupils to secure positions in some of the most prestigious colleges, universities, ensembles, orchestras and media organisations in the world.

Also unique is the commitment to all styles of music. Building on an exceptional reputation for classical teaching, the CEC Music School offers expertise in the fields of rock, jazz and traditional Scottish music. Exciting ventures have included workshops with internationally renowned singers, songwriters and instrumentalists, and lectures on the music industry. The Music School keeps abreast of all that is new on the music scene while ensuring the highest standards and finest traditions of teaching, performing and academic study.

Morgan Szymanski – 1998

'I came from The National School of Music in Mexico City. I heard about the Music School when I flew across to a guitar course in Wales. I am now studying classical and electric guitar, composition, music technology, piano and academic music. The City of Edinburgh Music School has been an important experience in my life – I had to leave my country and adapt to different culture. But thanks to the help and support from my teachers and other students, I feel I have settled in and am taking every opportunity to become the best musician possible. The only problem is the cold weather, which I find quite a shock to the system.'

After graduating in 2004 with First Class Honours and an M. Music from The Royal College of Music, London, Morgan embarked on a career as a soloist. He became the first solo guitarist to be selected for representation by the Young Concert Artists' Trust (YCAT), and in 2005 completed a series of recitals at the Wigmore Hall, London and concerts in Milan and Prague.

CONTINUED

Tommy Smith – 1983

Tommy is an international jazz saxophonist originally from Edinburgh. After studying at the Music School, Tommy received a scholarship to the prestigious Berklee College in Boston, USA. With his unique style of solo playing, he soon attracted the attention of jazz greats and embarked on several world tours. Television, radio and many magazine articles followed, and then the first record deal arrived with the famous Blue Note label. The albums *Step by Step*, *Peeping Tom*, *Standards* and *Paris* were released to great acclaim, and he is currently signed to Linn Records.

Tommy is also a composer of distinction. In 1990 he was commissioned by The Scottish Ensemble to write his first saxophone concerto and later a suite for sax and strings. Classical music continues to influence much of his music. Recently Tommy took a new direction, however, for a project-based album with Linn Records entitled *Beasts of Scotland*. Commissioned by the Glasgow International Jazz Festival, this idea was inspired by Edwin Morgan's poems and a series of paintings by Scottish artist Neil Bryce.

Maeve Gilchrist – 2003

'I joined The Music School when I was in primary 6, with the clarsach being my main instrument. An interest in singing grew and grew until jazz voice became my main interest. As well as this I gained Grade VIII on pedal harp, clarsach and Advanced Diploma on piano. I still love traditional Scottish music and have performed all over Scotland as well as being on the Music School's 'Blue Nova Sisters' CD and two other recent releases. Since joining the Music School I have performed at the opening of the Scottish Parliament, the Millennium Dome, and various festivals around Europe including Celtic Connections. I am now looking forward to continuing my studies at Berklee College of Music in Boston, USA.'

Maeve, following in the footsteps of Tommy Smith, was offered a generous scholarship to study jazz at Berklee and has travelled to New York, Milan and Barcelona to perform with her group.

USEFUL WEBSITES

Australian Institute of Sport: http//www.ais.org.au/
The Central Coast Academy of Sport (New South Wales, Australia):
http://www.thinksport.com.au/
Centre for Talented Youth, Johns Hopkins University: http://www.jhu.edu/~gifted/about/
The City of Edinburgh Music School: http://www.edinburghmusicschool.co.uk/
The Dance School of Scotland: http://www.knightswoodsecondary.org.uk/Danceschool
The Education Program for Gifted Youth (EPGY) at Stanford University, California:
http://www-epgy.stanford.edu/
The Irish Centre for Talented Youth: http://www.dcu.ie/ctyi/
The National Academy for Gifted and Talented Youth (NAGTY): http://www.nagty.ac.uk/
The Queensland Academy of Sport (QAS): http://www.qasport.qld.gov.au/
The Specialist Schools Trust: http://www.specialistschools.org.uk/
World Class Arena: http://worldclassarena.org
Young Concert Artists' Trust: http://www.ycat.co.uk

Chapter 11

Professional Development

This chapter looks at:

- Teacher training
- Advanced studies
- Electronic support

Some educators believe that gifted pupils do not need any specific provision; that truly gifted pupils will fulfil their educational needs on their own without any particular intervention, or that by offering an inclusive curriculum gifted pupils will make progress without the special attention needed by other atypical learners. But many teachers are concerned that they may ignore their gifted pupils' needs, not because they require less support, but because they have not been given any training in methods of identification and support.

TEACHER TRAINING

Many secondary teachers graduate in their subject specialism before going on to train as teachers; this training, including school placements, may leave little time for more than a brief glimpse of gifted educational provision. Newly qualified teachers are usually immersed in the demands of classroom management and the delivery of the subject curriculum, so may have less awareness of the needs of individual pupils unless they disrupt the learning environment. A small number of gifted pupils may deliberately do precisely that, and an inexperienced teacher is unlikely to interpret such behaviour as a response to boredom or lack of challenge and may even react by issuing sanctions or punishment exercises that offer even less challenge or stimulation. However, most gifted pupils will respond to lack of challenge by lowering their performance to the level expected and coast through the curriculum, probably developing poor study habits en route and effectively concealing their abilities from their subject teachers.

Education authorities often require newly qualified teachers to undertake additional professional training; many new teachers actively seek training opportunities to help them develop the skills they need in order to survive in the classroom. Professional development in gifted education at this stage might usefully focus on identifying giftedness and responding to underachievement; development of a differentiated subject curriculum; provision and management of enrichment opportunities; and effective programmes of group and individual acceleration.

At school level, induction programmes for new teachers should address gifted and talented issues, both at whole school and specific subject levels, to ensure that all teachers are informed of policy and of their duties to implement this in their classroom practice. School managers should ensure that teachers have access to training in meeting the needs of gifted and talented pupils not only in order to extend and deepen their knowledge and professional skills, but also to enable the planning and delivery of gifted and talented education in the school.

But the need for training does not stop at the classroom teacher level; the senior management team and any gifted-and-talented manager/co-ordinator should have received appropriate training; subject department heads and faculty leaders should have been given subject-specific training in managing strategies designed to meet the needs of gifted and talented pupils in their specialist area. Priorities for the development of gifted and talented provision should be embedded in the school's continuing professional development entitlement framework for all staff, and be monitored through evaluation and review procedures.

The need for additional teacher training is recognised around the world and is identified in government policy documents, national and local initiatives and by researchers and various groups and organisations committed to the development of gifted education.

For example, the Students with High Intellectual Potential (SHIP) Focus School Programme, a South Australian Department of Education and Children's Services (DECS) (1993–1997) initiative included in the planned outcomes for the SHIP Focus School Programme 1993–97:

- increased numbers of teachers trained in the identification of gifted students and the implementation of appropriate learning programmes for them;

- increased numbers of focus teachers, working collaboratively with SHIP co-ordinators in planning and facilitating training and development programmes for network schools;

- resource materials developed to support teacher training.

ADVANCED STUDIES

To support many such initiatives, post-graduate courses in the education of gifted children are offered to practising teachers by many universities, colleges and organisations around the world.

In Australia, at the University of New South Wales' Gifted Education Research Resource and Information Centre (GERRIC), a programme of studies was developed leading to post-graduate degrees specialising in gifted education and a Certificate in Gifted Education. Since 1991 teachers from every Australian state, New Zealand, Hong Kong and Vanuatu have successfully completed this.

In England, the Westminster Institute of Education, Oxford Brookes University offers continuing professional development courses for all those involved or interested in the education of gifted and talented learners specifically suited to the English educational system and integrated with other raising achievement strategies. Accredited courses include Teaching and Learning for Able/Gifted Pupils, and Able/Gifted Pupils – School-based Enquiry, as well as a National Training Programme for Gifted and Talented Co-ordinators. Also available to teachers on-line are professional development materials on gifted and talented provision and Launchpads, a series of briefing documents on specific aspects of gifted and talented education.

In Scotland, Strathclyde University offers an optional study *Able Pupils: Helping Them to Reach Their Full Potential* as part of the M.Sc. in Chartered Teacher Studies, while Glasgow University offers *More Able Pupils* as part of a distance learning post-graduate certificate course. The Scottish Network for Able Pupils (SNAP) associate tutor scheme provides training for those whose local authorities/organisations have joined the scheme and offers on-line reflection units (Glasgow University Interactive Distance Education – GUIDE) on gifted and talented education to teachers via their associate tutor.

Universities and colleges across the United States and Canada offer wide-ranging opportunities for practising teachers to take courses in gifted education, many leading to further certification. Some, like the National Research Center on the Gifted and Talented (a collaboration between the universities of Connecticut, Virginia and Yale) provide teachers with the opportunity to access current research and resources on-line. Others, notably the Johns Hopkins University's Center for Talented Youth and Stanford University's Educational Programs for Gifted Youth offer professional development opportunities for teachers as part of their programmes for young people. Many more conduct research while offering teachers post-graduate, masters and doctoral studies in gifted education, for example, the University of Connecticut's NEAG Centre for Gifted Education and Talent Development, and the Gifted Education Resource Institute (GERI) at Purdue University.

ELECTRONIC SUPPORT

The US National Association for Gifted Children, based in Washington, DC, offers a Professional Achievement Certificate where teachers are paired with an NAGC mentor who is a nationally recognised leader in the field of gifted and talented education to pursue a programme of advanced learning by following an individually tailored two-year programme culminating in a professional portfolio that demonstrates the teacher's expertise in four areas: knowledge, reflective understanding, problem solving and dissemination/service in an area related to gifted and talented education.

Teachers may also find support from the National Association for Able, Gifted and Talented Children (NACE), a charity, established in 1984 by members of the Schools Council Gifted Child Project to bring together and support all those with an interest in the education of able, gifted and talented children. NACE aims are to:

● Develop and exchange strategies for effective practice and further the professional development of members

● Provide professional responses to issues affecting education of able children and advice to government agencies

● Undertake development projects with partner organisations, local education authorities and groups of schools

● Provide professional expertise, advice, training and consultancy services, conferences, events, publications and resources

Teachers often have limited familiarity with the research on gifted education, and this, combined with a common belief that pupils do best remaining with their age group in order to be socially accepted, may lead to a neglect of the actual needs of gifted and talented pupils. Concerns about equality of provision for all and a worry that giving one pupil special provision might offend others, might prevent some teachers from providing appropriate learning experiences for their gifted pupils. If giftedness was viewed as a special educational need in much the same way as sensory or cognitive impairment, there might be a concerted effort to organise staff development and training that would support pupils' access to an appropriate curriculum. The Scottish Executive's Additional Support for Learning Act (2004) includes 'more able pupils' as a group that might have additional needs – firmly placing them alongside other 'special' categories.

No matter where gifted pupils are educated, they all need an appropriately differentiated curriculum designed to address their individual characteristics, needs, abilities, and interests with stimulating educational experiences appropriate to their level of ability. If teachers are offered development opportunities that equip them to modify the structure and organisation of the curriculum while employing a number of strategies for differentiation, enrichment and acceleration, they will be able to provide appropriate learning experiences for their gifted and talented pupils.

USEFUL WEBSITES

Gifted Education Resource Institute (GERI) at Purdue University: http://www.geri.soe. purdue.edu/profdev/default.html/

GERRIC: the University of New South Wales, Australia: http://www.arts.unsw.edu.au/gerric

Launchpads: http://www.brookes.ac.uk/schools/education/rescon/cpdgifted/launchpads

National Research Center on the Gifted and Talented at the University of Connecticut: http://www.gifted.uconn.edu/nrcgt.html

Centre for Talented Youth, Johns Hopkins University: http://www.jhu.edu/~gifted/about/

The National Association for Able, Gifted and Talented Children (NACE) http://www.nace.co.uk

The National Association for Gifted Children (NAGC) in Washington, DC: http://www.nagc. org/edcomm/pac.htm

Professional Achievement Certificate (PAC): http://www.nagc.org/edcomm/pac.htm

Scottish Network for Able Pupils (SNAP) http://www.ablepupils.com

Van Tassel-Baska, J. *Basic Educational Options for Gifted Students in Schools*: http://www.cfge. wm.edu/documents/Basic_Education_Options.htm

Westminster Institute of Education, Oxford Brookes University (cpdgifted): http://www. brookes.ac.uk/schools/education/rescon/cpdgifted/home.html

References

Branson, R. (2002) *Losing My Virginity: The Autobiography*. London: Virgin

Brockovich, E. and Eliot, M. (2001) *Take It from Me!: Life's a Struggle But You Can Win*. London: McGraw-Hill

Cademuir Consultancy (2003) *Scottish Enterprise Financial Services Team E-Mentoring Study*, electronic version retrieved on 4 May 2005 at http://www.scottish-enterprise.com/publications/e-mentoring_study

Clark, C. and Callow, R. (2002) *Educating the Gifted and Talented: Resource Issues and Processes for Teachers*, 2nd edn. London: Fulton. pp. 57–63

Colangelo, N., Assouline, S. and Gross, M.U.M. (2004) *A Nation Deceived: How Schools Hold Back America's Brightest Students*. The Templeton National Report on Acceleration. Iowa City, IA: University of Iowa, electronic version retrieved on 29 October 2004 at http://www.nationdeceived.org/

Colangelo, N. and Davis, G.A. (eds) (2003) *Handbook of Gifted Education*, 3rd edn. Boston, MD: Allyn and Bacon

Davis, R. (1994/1997) *The Gift of Dyslexia*. Burlingame, CA: Ability Workshop Press

De Bono, E. (1992) *Six Thinking Hats for Schools*. Cheltenham, Australia: Hawker Brownlow

Dracup, T. (2004) *New Directions in English Gifted and Talented Education*. Presentation at ECHA conference in Pamplona, Spain, September 2004, electronic version retrieved on 21 March 2005 at http://www.standards.dfes.giftedandtalented/downloads/powerpoint/echaslides.ppt#2

Duffy, S. (1999) *Eating Cake*. London: Sceptre

Duffy, S. (2000) *Immaculate Conceit*. London: Hodder & Stoughton

Education (Additional Support for Learning) (Scotland) Act 2004, electronic version retrieved on 21 July 2004 at http://www.scottish.parliament.uk/business/bills/pdfs/b11s2-aspassed

Eyre, D. (1997) *Able Children in Ordinary Schools*. London: Fulton. pp. 3, 16, 17–19, 38, 41, 108–9

Eyre, D. (2002a) 'Effective Schooling for the Gifted and Talented', in D. Eyre and H. Lowe, *Curriculum Provision for the Gifted and Talented in the Secondary School*. London: Fulton. pp. 13, 16, 17

Eyre, D. (2002b) *Structured Tinkering: Improving Provision for the Gifted in Ordinary Schools*, proceedings of the 8th Conference of the European Council for High Ability (ECHA), Rhodes, 9–13 October 2002, electronic version retrieved in March 2005 at http://www.warwick.ac.uk/gifted/professional-academy/professional-resources/documents/structured-tinkering

Eyre, D. (2004) *Gifted Education: The English Model*. National Academy for Gifted and Talented Youth, electronic version retrieved on 5 April 2005 at http://www.warwick.ac.uk/gifted/professional-academy/professional-resources/english-model.htm

Fisher, R. (2002) *Thinking Skills: Adding Challenge to the Curriculum*. A guide for teachers of able children. Glasgow: Scottish Network for Able Pupils.

Freeman, J. (1998) *Educating the Very Able: Current International Research*. London: The Stationery Office. pp. 4, 8–10, 24–5, 32, 34–5, 37–44, 44–7

Freeman, J. (2000) *The Education of the Very Able: Evidence as the Basis for Practice*. Presentation at the International Special Education Congress, Manchester, electronic version retrieved on 12 September 2004 at http://www.isec2000.org.uk/abstracts/papers_f/freeman_1.htm

Gagné, F. (1985) 'Giftedness and talent: a re-examination of the definitions', *Gifted Child Quarterly*, 29 (3): 103–12

Gagné, F. (2003a) 'High ability studies', *Journal of the European Council for High Ability*, 15 (2): 117–47

Gagné, F. (2003b) 'Transforming gifts into talents: the DMGT as a developmental theory', in N. Colangelo and G.A. Davis (eds), *Handbook of Gifted Education*, 3rd edn. Boston: Allyn and Bacon. pp. 60–74

Gallagher, S.A. and Gallagher, J.J. (2001) *Giftedness and Asperger's Syndrome: Sorting Through the Issues*. Presentation at the 14th Biennial Conference of the World Council for Gifted and Talented Children, Barcelona, August, electronic version retrieved on 6 April 2005 at http://www.worldgifted.org/xconfbar.htm

Gardner, H. (1993) *Frames of Mind: The Theory of Multiple Intelligences*, 10th edn. New York: Basic Books

George, D. (1995) *Gifted Education Identification and Provision*. London: Fulton. pp. 11, 12, 14

George, D. (1997) *The Challenge of the Able Child*, 2nd edn. London: Fulton. pp. 3–10, 35, 56, 93–5

George, D. (2000) *Gifted Education Identification and Provision*. London: Fulton. pp. 2, 3, 10–15, 30

Goddard, D. (2001a) *Gifted and Talented – Pack 1: Supporting Coordinators*. Cambridge: Pearson.

Goddard, D. (2001b) *Gifted and Talented – Pack 2: Involving Colleagues*. Cambridge: Pearson. pp. 40–55

Gross, M.U.M. (1989) 'The pursuit of excellence or the search for intimacy? The forced choice dilemma of gifted youth', *Roeper Review, A Journal on Gifted Education*, 11 (4): 189–94

Gross, M.U.M. (1998) 'The "me" behind the mask: intellectually gifted students and the search for identity', *Roeper Review, A Journal on Gifted Education*, 20 (3): 167–73

Gross, M.U.M. (2001) *Strategies to Help Reduce Underachievement in Academically Gifted Students*. Unpublished paper delivered to teachers in Edinburgh, October 2001.

Gross, M.U.M. (2004) *Exceptionally Gifted Children*, 2nd edn. London and New York: Routledge Falmer. pp. 6, 17, 24, 114, 145–8

Gross, M.U.M., MacLeod, B. and Pretorius, M. (2001) *Gifted Students in Secondary Schools Differentiating the Curriculum*, 2nd edn. Sydney, Australia: Gerric. pp. 2–8, 12–13, 31–44

Gross, M.U.M. and van Vliet, H.E. (2003) *Radical Acceleration of Highly Gifted Children: An annotated bibliography of international research on highly gifted young people who graduate from high school three or more years early*. Radnor, PA: John Templeton Foundation. pp. 11–12

Hagues, N. and Courtenay, D. (1993) *Verbal Reasoning*. Windsor: NFER-Nelson

Hagues, N. and Smith, P. (1993) *Non-Verbal Reasoning*. Windsor: NFER-Nelson

Heim, A.W., Watts, K.P. and Simmonds, V. (1970) *The AH Series of Tests*. Windsor: NFER-Nelson

Hendrickson, L. (1996) *Phenomenal Talent – The Autistic Kind*, electronic version retrieved on 17 April 2005 at http://www.nexus.edu.au/teachstud/gat/hendric1.htm

Honey, P. and Mumford, A. (1986) *The Manual of Learning Styles*. London: BBC Books

Hymer, B. and Michel, D. (2002) *Gifted and Talented Learners: Creating a Policy for Inclusion*. London: Fulton. pp. 21–48

Koshy, V. and Casey, R. (2000) *Special Abilities Scales: Observational Assessment for Identifying Able and High-Potential Students*. London: Hodder and Stoughton

Lohman, D.F., Hagen, E.P. and Thorndike, R.L. (2003) *Cognitive Abilities Test*, 3rd edn. Windsor: NFER-Nelson

McClure, L. (2001) 'Supporting the able mathematician', *Support for Learning*, 16 (1): 41–5

McGuinness, C. (1999) *From Thinking Skills to Thinking Classrooms: A Review and Evaluation of Approaches for Developing Pupils' Thinking*. Nottingham: DfEE Publications

McKay, N. (2004) 'Dyslexia and Inclusion: Generic strategies to meet diverse needs in mainstream settings'. Presentation at British Dyslexia Association International Conference in Warwick, March 2004, p. 2 of electronic version accessed in March 2006 at http://www.bdainternationalconference.org/2004/presentations/

McMichael, P. (1998) *Identifying Able Pupils: Report on Research Findings for the Scottish Network for Able Pupils (SNAP) Project*, Glasgow SNAP (under contract to SOEID). pp. 5, 19

Maker, C.J. (1982) *Curriculum Development for the Gifted*. Austin, TX: Pro-Ed.

Montgomery, D. (1996) *Educating the Very Able*. London: Cassell

Montgomery, D. (2003) *Gifted and Talented Children with Special Educational Needs*. London: NACE/Fulton. pp. 7, 8, 156, 160, 163

Moon, S.M. (2003) 'Personal talent', *High Ability Studies*, 14 (1): 5–21

Moon, S.M. (ed.) (2004) *Social/Emotional Issues, Underachievement, and Counseling of Gifted and Talented Students*. Thousand Oaks, CA: Corwin Press

Raven, J.C. (1938) *Raven's Progressive Matrices and Vocabulary Scales 8–14 Years*. Windsor: NFER-Nelson distributors

Reis, S.M. and J.S. Renzulli (undated) 'Curriculum Compacting: a systematic procedure for modifying the curriculum for above average ability students', The National Research Centre on the Gifted and Talents, University of Connecticut, electronic version accessed in March 2006 at http://www.sp.uconn.edu/~nrcgt/sem/semart08

Renzulli, J.S. (1988) 'The multiple menu model for developing differentiated curriculum for the gifted and talented', *Gifted Child Quarterly*, 32: 298–309

Renzulli, J.S. (1997a) *Five Dimensions of Differentiation*. Keynote presentation at the 20th Annual Confratute Conference, Storrs, CT in July.

Renzulli, J.S. (1997b) *Schools for Talent Development: A Practical Plan for Total School Improvement*. Mansfield Center, CT: Creative Learning Press

Renzulli, J.S. (1998) *A Rising Tide Lifts All Ships: Developing the Gifts and Talents of All Students*, electronic version at http://www.gifted.uconn.edu/sem/semart03.html

Renzulli, J.S. (1999) 'What is this thing called giftedness, and how do we develop it? A twenty-five year perspective', *Journal for the Education of the Gifted*, 23 (1): 3–54, electronic version retrieved on 4 October 2004 at http://www.sp.uconn.edu/~nrcgt/sem/semart14.html

Renzulli, J.S. (2000) 'Part 1: One way to organize exploratory curriculum academies of inquiry and talent development', *Middle School Journal*, 32 (1): 5–14

Renzulli, J.S. (undated) *A Practical System for Identifying Gifted and Talented Students*, electronic version accessed on 20 March 2006 at http://www.sp.uconn.edu/~nrcgt/sem/semart04.html

Renzulli, J.S. (2003) *A Bird's Eye View of The Schoolwide Enrichment Model: A Practical Plan for Total School Improvement*, condensed executive summary from J.S. Renzulli (1997b), electronic version at http://www.gifted.uconn.edu/sem/semexec.html

Renzulli, J. and Hartman, R. (1971) 'Scale for rating the behavioural characteristics of superior students', *Exceptional Children*, 38 (3): 243–8

Renzulli, J.S., Leppien, J.H. and Hays, T.S. (2000) *The Multiple Menu Model: A Practical Guide for Developing Differentiated Curriculum*. Mansfield Center, CT: Creative Learning Press, electronic version retrieved on 3 October 2004 at http://www.gifted.uconn.edu/mmm/pdfmmmjsr01.pdf

Renzulli, J.S. and Reis, S.M. (1997) *The Schoolwide Enrichment Model: A Comprehensive Plan for Educational Excellence*. Mansfield Center, CT: Creative Learning Press

Renzulli, J.S. and Richards, S. (2004) *Academies of Inquiry and Talent for the Middle School Years*. Seattle, WA: New Horizons for Learning, electronic version retrieved on 4 October 2004 at http://www.newhorizons.org/spneeds/gifted/renzulli%20richards

Riddell, L. (2005) *Fantasy Design, Children and Young People as Designers*. Helsinki: Writers and Design Museum. p. 79–80

Riley, T. (2004) 'Qualitative differentiation for gifted and talented students', in D. McAlipine and R. Moltzen (eds), *Gifted and Talented: New Zealand Perspectives*, 2nd edn. Palmerston North, NZ: Kanuka Grove

Riley, T., Bevan-Brown, J., Bicknell, B., Carroll-Lind, J. and Kearney, A. (2004) *The Extent, Nature and Effectiveness of Planned Approaches in New Zealand Schools for Providing for Gifted and Talented Students*. Wellington, NZ: New Zealand Ministry of Education. p. 11, electronic version retrieved on 12 May 2005 at http://www.minedu.govt.nz/

Rose, C. (1985) *Accelerated Learning*. New York: Dell.

Scottish Executive, The Curriculum Review Group (2004) *A Curriculum for Excellence*. Edinburgh: The Scottish Executive. pp. 14–15

Scottish Executive Education Department (2004) *Education (Additional Support for Learning) (Scotland) Act*. Edinburgh: The Stationery Office

Silverman, L.K. (1989) 'Invisible gifts, invisible handicaps', *Roeper Review*, 22 (1): 37–42

Smith, A. (1998) *Accelerated Learning in Practice*. Stafford: Network Educational. pp. 23–7, 37–56

Smith, A., Lovatt, M. and Wise, D. (2003) *Accelerated Learning: A User's Guide*. Stafford: Network Educational. p. 13

Smith, C.M., Barnes, S., Thomson, M., MacKenzie, T. and Cox, J. (2003) 'Local initiatives in Scotland', *Gifted Education International*, 18 (2): 194–200

Smith, C.M. and Doherty, M. (1998) *Identifying Abilities in Individual Curricular Areas*. Glasgow: SNAP. pp. 16–18, 19–40, 41–2, 43

Smith, P. and Lord, T.R. (2002) *Spatial Reasoning*. Windsor: NFER-Nelson

South Australian Department of Education and Children's Services (DECS) (1993–1997) *The Students with High Intellectual Potential (SHIP) Focus School Program*, electronic version retrieved on 9 June 2005 at http://www.nexus.edu.au/teachstud/gat/skabe1.htm

Starr, R. (2003) 'Show me the light – I can't see how bright I am: gifted students with visual impairment', in D. Montgomery (ed.), *Gifted and Talented Children with Special Educational Needs*. London: NACE/Fulton. p. 107

Sternberg, R.J. and Davidson, J. (eds) (1986) *Conceptions of Giftedness*. New York: Cambridge University Press

Sutherland, M. (2002) 'Identification of More Able Pupils: A Pilot Survey of Scottish Schools', *Gifted Education International*, 18 (2): 209–17

Teare, B. (1997) *Effective Provision for Able and Talented Children*. Stafford: Network Educational. pp. 65, 73–82

Teare, B. (1999) *Effective Resources for Able and Talented children*. Stafford: Network Educational Press

Teare, B. (2001) *More Effective Resources for Able and Talented Children*. Stafford: Network Educational Press

Van Tassel-Baska, J. (1989) 'Profiles of Preciosity – a three-year study of talented adolescents', in J. van Tassel-Baska and P. Olszewski-Kubilius (eds), *Patterns of Influence on Gifted Learners*. New York, NY: Teachers College Press. pp. 29–39

Van Tassel-Baska, J. (1992) 'Education decision making on acceleration and grouping', *Gifted Child Quarterly*, 36 (2): 68–72

Wallace, B. (2000) *Teaching the Very Able Child*. London: NACE/Fulton. pp. 7, 8

Wallace, B. and Adams, H.B. (1993) *Thinking Actively in a Social Context*. Oxford: AB Academic Publishers

Wallace, B. and Bentley, R. (eds) (2002) *Teaching Thinking Skills Across the Middle Years*. London: Fulton. pp. 4, 16–17, 45

Wang, M.C., Reynolds, M.C. and Walberg, H.J. (eds) (1991) *Handbook of Special Education: Research and Practice*, Vol. 4. Oxford: Pergamon

Webb, J.T., Amend, E.R. Webb, N.E., Goerss, J., Beljan P. and Olenchak, F.R. (eds) (2005) *Misdiagnosis and Dual Diagnoses of Gifted Children and Adults: ADHA, Bipolar, OCD, Asperger's, Depression, and Other Disorders*. Scottsdale, AZ: Great Potential Press

Welsh Assembly Government (2003) *Education Pupils Who Are More Able and Talented: Guidance for Local Education Authorities*, Cardiff Department for Training and Education consultation document, electronic version retrieved on 20 February 2005 at http://www.learning.wales.gov.uk/scripts/fe/news_details.asp?NewsID=848

West, T.G. (1997) *In the Mind's Eye*. New York: Prometheus

West, T.G. (1999) 'The abilities of those with reading disabilities: focusing on the talents of people with dyslexia', in D.D. Duane (ed.), *Reading and Attention Disorders: Neurobiological Correlates*. New York, NY: York Press, electronic version posting dated 1 November 2000, retrieved on 16 April 2005 at http://www. ldonline.org/article.php?max=20&id=699&loc=76

Williams, S. (2004) 'Taking the Right Steps', *Teaching Thinking and Creativity* (14): 5–11

Winstanley, C. (2003) 'Gifted children with hearing impairment', in D. Montgomery (ed.), *Gifted and Talented Children with Special Educational Needs*. London: NACE/Fulton. p. 115

Index